NALANDA

ADVANCE PRAISE FOR THE BOOK

'Abhay K. has written a wonderfully accessible introduction to early India's most important centre of philosophy and learning, the great monastery—university of Nalanda. Setting his story within a seductively sketched panorama of the golden age of early Buddhism, Abhay celebrates Nalanda's dazzling libraries, scholars, teachings, doctrines and finally, its global influence. Sympathetic, scholarly and poetic, Abhay K's *Nalanda* fills an important gap and deserves to be widely read'—**William Dalrymple, writer and historian**

'Even as he resurrects Nalanda from the embers of history, Abhay K. does not simply eulogize it; instead, he transforms this wellspring of scholastic endeavour into an emblem of humankind's quest for knowledge. In my view, Abhay K's *Nalanda*, stunning and scholarly, is an outstanding starting point'—**Shashi Tharoor, writer and member of Parliament**

'Abhay K's evocative telling brings the layered history of Nalanda to life. The hallowed centre of learning for over a millennium, the Mahavihara first nurtured the idea of the university, and left an indelible imprint on global thought'—**Namita Gokhale, author and festival director, Jaipur Literature Festival**

'Son of the soil Abhay K. tells the story of Nalanda Mahavihara's revered scholars, groundbreaking philosophies and the vibrant life within the world's first residential university. He traces how it shaped the intellectual landscape of its era, influencing generations of thinkers and spiritual leaders'—**Rana Safvi, writer and historian**

'For 700 years, Nalanda was considered the greatest university globally. Attracting students and grants from around the world, it would have been the envy of a modern Ivy League. In his simple and readable style, Abhay K. puts together what is known about this remarkable institution from a range of sources'—**Sanjeev Sanyal, writer and economist**

NALANDA

How It Changed the World

ABHAY K.

VINTAGE
An imprint of Penguin Random House

PENGUIN VINTAGE

Penguin Vintage is an imprint of the Penguin Random House group of companies whose
addresses can be found at global.penguinrandomhouse.com

Published by Penguin Random House India Pvt. Ltd
4th Floor, Capital Tower 1, MG Road,
Gurugram 122 002, Haryana, India

Penguin
Random House
India

First published in Penguin Vintage by Penguin Random House India 2025

ISBN 9780670099627

Typeset in Adobe Garamond Pro by MAP Systems, Bengaluru, India
Printed at Replika Press Pvt. Ltd, India

www.penguin.co.in

MIX
Paper | Supporting
responsible forestry
FSC™ C016779

Contents

Introduction

'There is no clear and entirely reliable interpretation of Nalanda's past or, for that matter, the past of just about anything. Rather, there are scattered ideas that we try to string together as history, an overview stitched from snippets. And there is no single interpretation of these snippets but rather competing and conflicting interpretations. Recognizing this—the slippery nature of the past and its documents—is part of what makes scholarship such an exciting enterprise.'[1]

Buddhist monasteries existed all over India, Central Asia and East Asia. However, Nalanda became a celebrated monastery in comparison to its contemporaries. What might be the reason?

One of the reasons was its proximity to Rajagriha (modern Rajgir), the first capital of Magadha. Rajagriha in those days was full of political intrigue and rivalries. It became a fertile ground for the birth of the Magadha empire. Over the centuries, Magadha was ruled by a succession of dynasties, including the Brihdratha dynasty, the Pradyota dynasty and the Haryanka dynasty. The Haryanka dynasty was the third ruling dynasty of Magadha. It was founded by Bimbisara (c. 558–c.491 BCE). He is considered to be a contemporary of both Mahavira (c. 599–527 BCE) and Gautama Buddha (c. 563–483 BCE). His son Ajatashatru further consolidated it after forcefully taking over Magadha from his father and imprisoning him. He fought a war against the Vajjika League, led by the Licchavis, and conquered the republic of Vaishali. He laid the foundations of the city of Pataliputra by fortifying a village on the southern bank of the Ganges to have better control over the Licchavis.

Ajatashatru followed an expansionist policy and defeated his neighbours, including the king of Kosala. His brothers, who also claimed the throne of Magadha, took refuge in Kashi, the capital of Kosala. It led to a war between Magadha and Kosala. Ajatashatru conquered Kashi and captured the other smaller kingdoms in the Gangetic plains. Magadha under Ajatashatru became the most powerful kingdom in North India. He was a strategist and an innovator of new weapons and is credited with the invention of the *rathamusala* (a scythed chariot) and the *mahashilakantaka* (an engine to eject large sized stones).

Rajagriha played a significant role in the Buddha's life. After leaving his father's palace in Kapilvastu, the Buddha first visited Vaishali and then Rajagriha. He spent time in solitude in the Pandava hills at Rajagriha and later begged for alms in its streets, attracting many with his calm demeanour. Here, the Buddha met his five ascetic companions, who later received the first Dhamma sermon at Sarnath after his enlightenment.

King Bimbisara of Magadha met Siddhartha Gautama and invited him to stay at his palace. However, Gautama declined Bimbisara's offer and proceeded towards the ancient city of Gaya. He attained enlightenment at Bodh Gaya and gave his first sermon at Sarnath, after which he returned to Rajagriha. He was received with great fanfare by King Bimbisara at the city gates and was escorted to the royal capital where Bimbisara gifted him the Venuvana, the royal bamboo grove. The Buddha met Shariputra and Maudgalyayana, at Rajagriha, who later became his chief disciples. Both hailed from Nalanda.

The Buddha often meditated at the Griddhakuta Parvat in Rajagriha and gave some of his most important sermons there. It is believed that Bodhisattva Avalokiteshvara propounded the *Prajnaparamitahṛdaya* or *The Heart of Perfection of Wisdom* or *Heart Sutra* to Shariputra in the presence of the Buddha at the Griddhakuta Parvat. Its first line states: 'Form is emptiness (Shunyata), emptiness is form.' It conveys that ultimately all phenomena are empty (shunya) of inherent existence. It is the most frequently used and recited text in the Mahayana Buddhist tradition. The *Heart Sutra* has been translated into English dozens of times from Chinese, Sanskrit, Tibetan and other languages. The last line of the Heart Sutra, which is its essence, is often recited by Mahayana Buddhists: '*gate gate paragate parasaṃgate bodhi svaha*'. It can be translated as 'gone, gone, gone beyond, beyond all, enlightened.'

Shariputra, who was born at Nalanda, came from a family engaged in scholarly debates for generations and, as per the legend, his family had inherited the village of Nalanda as a trophy for winning scholarly debates at Rajagriha.

The lives of Nalanda's legendary sons, Shariputra and Maudgalyayana, are noteworthy for their spiritual quest and the role they played in the evolution of Buddhism. They became *arhants*—the highest stage of nirvana in Theravada Buddhism—and continue to inspire to this day a legion of followers across the world.

As the first chief disciple, Shariputra's role was to organize the Buddha's teachings systematically. His mastery in teaching the Buddha Dharma earned him the nickname 'the General of the Dharma' (*Dharmasenapati*). The Buddhist Sangha was led by Shariputra. He routinely doubled up for the Buddha himself while discharging the affairs of the Sangha, including ordaining new monks.

The second chief disciple of the Buddha, Maudgalyayana, was a very popular teacher. To honour Maudgalyayana, the Buddha instructed that an image depicting *Bhavachakra*, the Wheel of Becoming be painted at the gate of Venuvana and the law of Karma be explained to all the visitors. It is believed that Maudgalyayana was responsible for creating the first Buddha image, the Udayana Buddha. He was killed by robbers presumably hired by a rival sect, at Rajagriha.

Shariputra achieved his nirvana at Nalanda. To honour him, the Mauryan emperor Ashoka built a stupa at Nalanda. Next to it he constructed a *vihara* for the Buddhist monks, which evolved into Nalanda Mahavihara in centuries to come.[2]

From the late fourth century onwards, Nalanda received royal patronage from the imperial Guptas. The copper plate inscription of Samudragupta (c. 350–375 CE) issued in his fifth regnal year, mentions the donation of a village named Pushkaraka to Nalanda sangharama. Kumargupta I (c. 415–455 CE) built a sangharama near the Great Stupa of Shariputra, and Skandagupta (c. 455–467 CE), Purugupta (c. 467–473 CE) and Narasimhagupta Baladitya (c. 495–530 CE) also built viharas and temples at Nalanda. Later, Harshavardhana (c. 606–647 CE) built monasteries and temples at Nalanda and granted revenue of 200 villages to the Mahavihara.[3]

The kings of the Pala dynasty, such as Gopala (c. 750–770 CE), Dharmapla (c. 770–810 CE), and Mahipala (c. 988–1038 CE) were the last great patrons of Buddhism in India, whose donation inscriptions to Nalanda Mahavihara have been found during excavations.

From the third century BCE to the early fourteenth century CE, Nalanda was the seat of several great scholars who made significant contributions in various fields such as science, medicine, public health, mathematics, astronomy, philosophy, logic, art, architecture, translation, poetry, script, grammar and religion, among others. Some of these great luminaries of Nalanda include Nagarjuna (c. 1st–3rd century CE), the foremost thinker in Mahayana Buddhism who advocated the *Madhyamaka* philosophy of emptiness; Aryadeva (c. 3rd century CE), the most important philosopher in the Madhyamaka school of thought after Nagarjuna; Asanga (c. 4th century CE) and Vasubandhu (c. 4th–5th century CE), the two brothers from Gandhara, the proponents of the *Yogachara* school of Buddhist philosophy; Buddhapalita (c. 470–550 CE), one of the great commentators on Nagarjuna's Madhyamaka philosophy; Aryabhata (c. 476–550 CE), the father of Indian mathematics and the first person to assign zero as a digit, which simplified mathematical computations and led to the evolution of algebra and calculus; Dinnaga (c. 480–540 CE), one of the founders of Buddhist logic; Chandrakirti (c. 600–650 CE), a noted Buddhist scholar who wrote an extensive commentary on the works of Nagarjuna and Aryadeva; Sthiramati (c. 6th century CE), a Buddhist scholar, who along with Gunamati, founded the monastery of Vallabhi in Gujarat; Dharmapala (c. 530–561 CE), who headed Nalanda Mahavihara during a critical time; Shilabhadra (c. 529–645 CE), the head of Nalanda Mahavihara when Xuanzang visited the monastery and a great scholar of Yogachara philosophy; Dharmakirti (c. 6th–7th century CE), a major figure in advancing Buddhist philosophy; Vajrabodhi, a great Vajrayana master who travelled to China as an envoy of the Pallava monarch to the Tang emperor; Shantarakshita (c. 725–788 CE), who helped King Trisong Detsen to establish Tibet's first Buddhist monastery, named Samaye; Padmasambhava (c. 8th–9th century CE) or Guru Rimpoche, founder of the Nyingma sect—the oldest of the four major schools of Tibetan Buddhism; Kamalashila (c. 740–795 CE), who established Lamaism and Tantric Buddhism in Tibet; Chandrogomin (c. 8th century CE), a Tantra master; Dharmadeva (c. 973–1001 CE), a monk at Nalanda Mahavihara who went to China and translated forty-six Sanskrit works during the period 973–981; Atisha (c. 982-1054 CE), the head of Nalanda Mahavihara and Buddhakirti (11th–12th century) and Dhyanabhadra (c. 1289–1363 CE) who played a key role in spreading Mahayana Buddhism in early 14th century in East Asia, perhaps the last great scholar of Nalanda Mahavihara before it was abandoned, among others.

Nalanda became a renowned centre of learning because of these great scholars. As a celebrated and reputed seat of learning, Nalanda Mahavihara attracted many foreign scholars who came to study and copy various Buddhist sutras from its famous library. Xuanzang and Yijing from China are the two most well-known foreign scholars who played a vital role in chronicling and preserving the glorious history of Nalanda.

During the reign of emperor Taizong of the Tang dynasty, Xuanzang travelled across India (630–643 CE) and spent five years at Nalanda. He was warmly welcomed at Nalanda Mahavihara, where he received the Indian moniker Mokshadeva and studied Yogachara philosophy under the mentorship of Shilabhadra, the venerable head of the institution at the time. Moreover, he also took courses in grammar, logic and Sanskrit and later taught at the Mahavihara. He carried 657 Buddhist texts along with him to China when he returned and left behind a detailed account of the time he spent in Nalanda—

'An azure pool winds around the monasteries, adorned with the full-blown cups of the blue lotus; the dazzling red flowers of the lovely *kanaka* hang here and there, and outside groves of mango trees offer the inhabitants their dense and protective shade.[4]'

Inspired by the journey of Xuanzang, I wrote a poem:

A half-monk at thirteen
restless to find the truth
one night I saw in my dream

an azure pool
a blue lotus
dazzling red flowers

thick mango groves
the wrinkled face of a Bhikchhu
I set out for Yintu

secretly escaping the Middle Kingdom
at night, like the young Siddhartha
against the Emperor's diktats

I travelled alone for years
a fakir on the northern route
hungry, naked but blessed

crossing Gobi, Tien Shan,
Samarkand, Jalandhar, Kashmir,
Kannauj, Varanasi, Pataliputra

On my way I met kings and queens
saw blossoming monasteries;
decaying, crumbling ruins

Finally, I found Nalanda
hidden as a jewel
under the thick mango groves

Silbhadra had always known
I would come to Nalanda
as a bee comes to a flower seeking nectar

He took me in as one of his own
taught me Yogachara
and gave me a new name, Mokshadeva

Spending many blissful years
with the Guru and fellow monks
I absorbed their profound wisdom

set out to travel across the moon land
visiting Kanchipuram, Ajanta, Malva, Multan
Nostalgic, I returned to Nalanda

before bidding a final farewell
to head for Kamrupa, the land of Brahmaputra
ruled by the learned Kumar Bhaskar Varman

but my friend King Harshavardhan
could not bear my absence for long
I was brought to attend the Great Assembly at Kannauj

extolled Mahayana Buddhism there, visited Prayag
then journeyed home, my horses laden with texts,
statues, rare relics of the Enlightened One

I nearly drowned crossing the Indus
washed away by its mighty currents
but was saved by local fishermen

Continuing my journey back
passing Khyber, Kashgar, Khotan,
arriving in Chang'an where

a great procession celebrated my return
the Emperor himself at the city gates
welcomed me with open arms

showered on me
the highest honours of the land
but gently I refused them all

I presented Emperor Taizong
my Great Tang Records (On Western Regions)
and retired to the monastery at Da Ci'en

translating precious gems
gathered on my odyssey
to the Buddha's pure land.

'Xuanzang successfully petitioned the Tang Emperor for a Nalanda-like Tower of Sanskrit scriptures to protect the manuscripts he had brought back. The result was the Great Wild Goose Pagoda, a 210-foot-tall spectacular sutra library that still stands in Xi'an today.[5]' 'Empress Wu Zetian commissioned a stunning colossal 55-foot-high image of Vairocana Buddha introduced to China by the Tantric Buddhist texts brought from Nalanda by Xuanzang.' His adventures inspired Wu Cheng'en's sixteenth century novel, *Journey to the West*, which refers to India as 'Buddha's pure land'.

Unlike Xuanzang, Yijing came to India via the sea route. He arrived in India in the seventh century (673 CE) and stayed for fourteen years, spending most of these years at Nalanda Mahavihara. When he returned to China in 695, he carried with him 400 Sanskrit manuscripts, which were subsequently translated into Mandarin. Empress Wu Zetian gave him a grand welcome. Yijing's account mainly focused on the practice of Buddhism in India and detailed descriptions of the life of the monks at the monastery.

His main purpose to visit India was to improve the practice of monastic rules in Chinese–Buddhist monasteries by copying the rules followed at Indian monasteries. He stayed at Nalanda for ten years (675–685) and recorded the customs and way of life of the monks and teachers at Nalanda Mahavihara. In his *Memoirs of Eminent Monks who Visited India and Neighboring Regions in Search on the Law during the Great Tang Dynasty*, Yijing highlights that Chinese Buddhist monks visited India in large numbers despite the perilous nature of the journey. Some returned to China while many died during their return journey or stayed back in India. His memoir provides short accounts of the lives of fifty-six monks who visited India in the seventh century, highlighting the zeitgeist among them to visit Buddhist sites and study at Nalanda. Some prominent ones included Hyecho, Hui-yieh and Aryavarma from Korea; Tao Hsi and Wu-hsing from China and Bodhidharma from Tukhara (Bactria), among others.

As mentioned by Xuanzang in his travel accounts, Buddhism was in decline in India after the seventh century CE, except in Bihar and Bengal, where it received royal patronage. The tantric practices in Buddhism in Eastern India were becoming more pronounced and causing resentments. Also, Brahmanism was on the rise because Vajrayana resembled the ritualistic practices of Hinduism.

The Gangetic plains of Magadha were undergoing political turmoil and a power vacuum after the decline of the Pala dynasty in the twelfth century, which led to drying up of the sources of continued royal patronage to Nalanda Mahavihara. This unstable situation was effectively exploited by the foreign invaders and their military commanders, especially Bakhtiyar Khalji and his troops, who started raiding the rich Buddhist monasteries of Magadha.

Persian historian Minhaj-i-Siraj Juzjani (1193-1266 CE), in his work titled *Tabaqat-i-Nasiri*, an elaborate history of the Islamic world completed in 1260, writes that Khalji attacked the fortified city of Odantapuri, considered to be the present day Bihar Sharif in 1197. Based on this, it is assumed that Bakhtiyar Khalji also attacked and looted Nalanda, which was located nearby and was the most reputed and the richest of all the Buddhist monasteries. Nalanda suffered immensely from Khalji's military invasion, plunder and loot; however, Nalanda was too large to be completely destroyed in one invasion. Khalji looted several Buddhist monasteries and temples. He even planned to loot the rich monasteries of Tibet to amass more wealth; however, he failed in his mission and was killed by his own lieutenant commander in 1206.

Nalanda Mahavihara was again raided by the troops of the Turkish military commander stationed at Odantapuri in 1235 as per the accounts of the Tibetan monk Dharmasvamin, who visited Nalanda from 1234–1236.

I have written a poem about the raid of Nalanda:

The Day of Massacre at Nalanda

Bakhtiyar and his men
play buzkashi in my alleys today

monks are being burnt alive; and
those who try to escape are beheaded.

Dharamganj—the nine storied library
has burst into flames

smoke and ash from burning books
have turned the day into night

The sun has disappeared from the sky today
and even my bricks bleed,

sacred chants that once purified Magadha
have turned into shrieks of a falling humanity

The light of the world is fading today
to face the ravages of time alone

abandoned, scorned, forgotten
or perhaps, to be reborn into many Nalandas.

Though the edifices of Nalanda were largely reduced to mounds and the great monastery ceased to function in the early fourteenth century—its legacy in the development of Science, Medicine, Mathematics, Astronomy, Philosophy, Logic, Grammar, Script, Book Culture, Translation, Language, Literature, Art and Architecture among others endures to this day.

The first Vihara at Nalanda was founded in the third century BCE by Emperor Ashoka.[6] A standard architectural plan of the vihara developed as a residential seat of learning during the Mauryan period and attained a regular form at Nalanda Mahavihara, which is considered to have inspired the courtyard structure of colleges and universities across Europe, including the quads and courts of Oxford and Cambridge University.

The evolution of Nalanda from a Vihara founded in the third century BCE into a Mahavihara with a well laid out plan with multiple monasteries, a developed infrastructure, large endowments, a walled residential campus, multiple rectangular monasteries, international students, where a variety of disciplines, including secular disciplines, were taught by the best scholars of their time, is how the idea of a university evolved in its true sense over centuries and spread to Central Asia, Europe and the rest of the world.

Great scholars such as Nagarjuna, Vasubandhu, Shantarakshita and Kamalashila at Nalanda Mahavihara contributed greatly to advancing the recursive argument method—an argument followed by sub-arguments, which led to the development of the medieval scientific method. This approach spread to different parts of the world, including Central Asia, and eventually reached to the Arab world and Europe.

Aryabhata, who is regarded as the 'father of Indian mathematics', was the most prominent mathematician at the Nalanda Mahavihara in the sixth century CE. The author of his seminal book *Aryabhatia*, he was the first mathematician to assign zero as a digit, a revolutionary concept, which simplified mathematical computations and gave birth to concepts which later became known as algebra and calculus.

Brahmgupta later improved the work of Aryabhata and wrote *Brahmasphuṭasiddhanta,* which was translated into Arabic in the eighth century and became widely known as *Sindhind*, which in turn introduced Indian numbers, algebra, calculus, algorithm and Indian astronomy to Europe. Nalanda's impact in the field of mathematics and astronomy was particularly significant in China.

Nalanda contributed to the development and evolution of two major Mahayana Buddhist philosophies viz. Madhyamaka and Yogachara. The continuous engagement with Yogachara for centuries at the Mahavihara led to the evolution of a specialized school known as Vajrayana or Tantrayana, based on the principles of Yogachara philosophy.

A new philosophy, synthesizing Madhyamaka and Yogachara, was developed at Nalanda Mahavihara by Shantarakshita, which is known as *Yogachara–Madhyamaka.*

Nalanda Mahavihara played a key role in the spread of these Nalanda-grown philosophies across South, Central, East and South-East Asia, shaping the cultural and religious perspective of the people in the countries of these regions. The bronze art of Nalanda had an impact on the art of East, South and Southeast Asian countries.

'The development of the quadrangular vihara and the formation of the *panchayatan chaitya* remains Nalanda's foremost contribution to the sphere of architecture.'[7]

The idea of making three-dimensional mandalas evolved with the Tantric Buddhist principles developed at Nalanda Mahavihara as part of the Vajrayana philosophy, which was used to build the Buddhist stupas of Kesariya in Bihar and Borobudur in Java, the world's largest Buddhist monument.

The acharyas of Nalanda enriched Sanskrit language by composing their works in Sanskrit, which included philosophical texts, compositions on Buddhist logic and ethical manuals in pure and Panini Sanskrit, and *stotras, mahatmyas, dharanis, tantras* and *sadhnas* in hybrid Sanskrit.

The great tradition of translation at Nalanda Mahavihara enriched the language, literature and culture of many countries over centuries. The culture and language of Tibet is a living testimony to this tradition.

The Tibetan scholar Thonmi Sambhota, who studied at Nalanda Mahavihara, devised scripts for the Tibetan language based on the Gupta Brahmi script.

Eighty-four Siddhas of Nalanda Mahavihara, along with the Jain saints, played a pivotal role in the development of *Apabhramsa* poetry from the eighth to the thirteenth century, contributing to new poetic forms such as *doha, chaupai* and *paddhari* among others.

Nalanda played a central role in developing the art of manuscript writing, illustration, preservation and copying. Thus, manuscript writing, copying and preservation culture at Nalanda accelerated the transition from an oral culture to a writing culture worldwide.

The world's first printed book is *The Diamond Sutra*, a part of *Prajnaparamita Sutra*, believed to be written by Nagarjuna at Nalanda. The Dhamma Wheel, in which the sacred texts are mechanically revolved, was invented at Nalanda. Medicine practice at Nalanda greatly impacted the medical tradition of East Asia, especially China, including advanced ophthalmology practised at Nalanda, which was introduced to Tang China.

The Rasaratnakara, composed by Nagarjuna in the early centuries CE, is considered the first treatise on Indian alchemy.

Nalanda's excellence and best practices in medicine, ophthalmology, alchemy and other health sciences were embraced in Tibet, Nepal, China, Korea, Japan, Mongolia and many parts of the world.

The life and ideals of Jesus Christ have a close parallel with the Buddha taking birth as Bodhisattvas and sacrificing his own life to save others in the Jataka Tales. The scholastic tradition at Nalanda developed by Nagarjuna popularized the view that these Bodhisattvas were at par with the historical Buddha himself. Several historians believe that there is a real possibility that Buddhism influenced the early development of Christianity.

Though Nalanda Mahavihara ceased to exist in the early fourteenth century, its great fame continued to live and inspire the establishment of monasteries and educational institutions named after it. The legend of Nalanda lives on and has gathered pace in recent years.

Nava Nalanda Mahavihara was founded in 1951 in Nalanda, Bihar and attached to it is a memorial hall dedicated to the great Chinese traveller Xuanzang, which was completed in 1984. Karma Shri Nalanda Institute was founded in 1981 in Sikkim and Nalanda Open University was established in 1987 at Nalanda, Bihar.

In 2006, Dr A.P.J. Abdul Kalam proposed the idea for the revival of Nalanda Mahaviahara. In 2007, the Bihar Legislative Assembly passed a bill for the creation of a new university. Nalanda Mentor Group (NMG), led by Nobel Laureate Amartya Sen, was set up in 2007 with the aim of promoting the idea of the establishment of Nalanda University. The proposal was formally endorsed at the second East Asia summit in 2007. The government of India passed the Nalanda University Bill in 2010, establishing Nalanda University. Here is my poetic homage on the rise of Nalanda after 700 years in its homeland—

The Rise of Nalanda

Forlorn under the red earth
buried for centuries
I rise today like a phoenix,
seven hundred years later
from the ashes of my burnt books.

I open my arms today to embrace you
whoever you are, from wherever you are
come, walk into my enlightened fold
as once the Buddha and Mahavira did
seeking shelter in my groves.

I remember Yijing and Xuanzang–
the saint-seekers from the East,
I hear the footsteps of Aryabhata
in my ancient compound today
you too come; come as I rise again.

Nalanda's reputation in foreign lands led to the establishment of several institutions named after it. Nalanda Gedige in Sri Lanka dates to the eighth century, when Nalanda Mahavihara was still functioning.

Phenpo Nalendra, a Tibetan Nalanda Monastery was founded in 1435 in the Phen-yul valley, to the north-east of Lhasa, by the monk-scholar Rongton Sheja Kunrig (1347–1449). It housed approximately 700 resident monks and thousands of visiting monks and has branches in various parts of Tibet.

In Europe, a Nalanda Monastery was founded at Lavaur, about forty kilometers from Toulouse, France, in 1981, by Lama Zopa Rinpoche and Lama Thubten Yeshe.

In 1989, Nalanda Buddhist Centre was opened in Brazil while a decade later in 1999, Nalandarama Retreat Centre was established in Brazil. In 2000, Nalanda College of Buddhist Studies was started in Toronto in Canada. The same year the International Buddhist College (IBC) was founded in Hatyai, Thailand. In 2007, Nalanda Institute was founded Kuala Lumpur, Malaysia.

Nalanda Institute, founded in 2007 on the southern outskirts of Kuala Lumpur, Malaysia, was modelled after Nalanda Mahavihara to promote Buddhist studies in the country.

Nalanda Institute for Contemplative Science was founded in the USA by Joe Loizzo, a psychiatrist in 2007, who was inspired by the ancient university of Nalanda. It was conceptualized during his research in contemplative science at Columbia University and Weill Cornell Medical College from 1996.

As evident from these examples of Nalanda's growing footprints in Asia, Europe, North and South America and Australia, it is clear that the repute of Nalanda is going to grow in times to come. Nalanda's age old tradition of imparting knowledge, wisdom and kindness can help humanity in overcoming hatred, anger, frustration, greed and in achieving inner and outer peace.

On a personal note, I was born and raised in the Nalanda district of Bihar. Yet much about Nalanda was a mystery to me. It was during my school days that I started exploring the ruins of the Nalanda Mahavihara.

I used to climb Griddhakuta Parvat in Rajgir to get a panoramic view of the hills and forests surrounding it but was unaware of its great significance for Buddhists the world over. Since the time

I first read the powerful *Heart Sutra*, I often recite its first and last lines. I think about Faxian spending a night at Griddhakuta Parvat or Yijing dreaming to build a second Rajagriha in his homeland, China. I recall memories of beautiful days I spent in Rajgir, meditating on the Vulture peak.

I was thrilled to find a poet in Yijing, who would often break into verse whenever he came across a fellow monk who had left this world or to mark a high moment in his life. I have cherished reading his poems and observations about Nalanda and Rajgir.

Writing this book has been a steep learning curve for me and has given me immense pleasure.

I often go back to the new campus of Nalanda University, which has been newly built in Rajgir. It was one of my childhood dreams to see Nalanda rising from its ruins and I am fortunate to see it happening in my lifetime. The exquisite architecture of Nalanda University reminds me of Nalanda Mahavihara, especially its red bricks. It's six-storey library resembles Nalanda's renowned Dharmaganja Library. I wish to see the lecture halls, auditoriums, ponds, buildings at the Nalanda University to be named after the great luminaries of Nalanda Mahavihara or their famous works, as well as the international scholars who visited it, to keep their memories alive. We have already paid the price of historical amnesia, of forgetting about Nalanda and its heritage. Let's not allow it to happen again.

May the rise of Nalanda create a new consciousness and solidarity among people across the planet and may many more Xuanzangs visit Nalanda once again.

1

Nalanda: A Suburb of Rajagriha, the First Capital of Magadha

'There were monasteries all over India, so we need to ask why Nalanda achieved the distinction it did; why this great monastery rather than one of the others at Vikramashila, Uddandapura, Somapura (better known by its modern name, Paharpur) and Jagaddala. In part, the answer is its location.'—Frederick M. Asher

According to the Jaina text, *Sutrakritanga,* Nalanda was a suburb (*bahiriya*) situated to the north-west of the famous city of Rajagriha (modern Rajgir). Rajgir is situated about 100 km to the south-east of Patna in the Nalanda district of Bihar. Bihar Sharif (the district headquarters) is situated about 35 km north-east of Rajgir, and 22 km north-west of it is the sacred site of Pavapuri, where Mahavira attained nirvana. Nalanda is about 16 kilometres north of the city of Rajgir, about 90 kilometres south-east of Patna and about 80 kilometres north-east of Bodh Gaya.

The *Mahaparinibbanasutta* of the *Digha Nikaya* mentions Rajagriha among six great cities at the time of the Buddha. It was an important trade centre as it played a significant role in long-distance trade with Takshila, Mathura, Kausambi, Varanasi, Gaya,

1

Pataliputra, and the Tamralipti/Kalinga region, supplying raw materials sourced from the Chota Nagpur plateau area, especially from the mining sites of Koderma.

The Jains believe that the twentieth Trithankara, Muni Suvrata, was born at Rajagriha. The twenty-fourth and last Jain Trithankara, Mahavira, spent as many as fourteen *varshas* (rainy seasons) here. The early Buddhist records refer to six heterodoxical ideologues such as Purana Kassapa, Gosala, Pakudha Kaccayana, Ajita, Sanjaya Belatthiputra and Nigantha Nataputta having a strong presence in Rajagriha, each with their own set of followers.

It was the period of intense power rivalry among the *mahajanapadas* (great kingdoms) of North India, with Magadha's power continually rising, especially under the reigns of kings Bimbisara and Ajatashatru.

Bimbisara was the son of Bhattiya, a chieftain, who was defeated by the king of Anga. He ascended to the throne at the age of fifteen, in 543 BCE and established the Haryanka dynasty in Magadha. Bimbisara's first capital was Rajagriha. He led a military campaign against Anga to avenge his father's earlier defeat at the hands of its king, Brahmadatta. The campaign was successful, Anga was annexed, and Prince Kunika (Ajatashatru) was appointed governor of Champa, the capital of Anga. His conquest of Anga gave Magadha control over the routes to the Ganges delta, which had important ports that gave Magadha access to the eastern coast of India. Bimbisara entered into marriage alliances to strengthen his power. His first wife was Kosala Devi, the daughter of Maha Kosala, the king of Kosala and sister of Prasenajit. As a dowry, he was given Kashi. This marriage alliance ended the hostility between Magadha and Kosala and made way for him to subjugate other neighbouring mahajanapadas.

His second wife, Chellana, was a Licchavi princess from Vaishali and the daughter of the Jain king Chetaka, and his third wife was the Vaishali princess, Vasavi.

The relations between the Licchavis and their southern neighbour, the kingdom of Magadha, were initially good; nevertheless, there were occasional tensions between the two states. Later, when the Licchavis invaded Magadhi territory from across the Ganges, their relations deteriorated permanently.

The hostilities between the Licchavis and Magadha continued under the rule of Ajatashatru—Bimbisara's son from the second Licchavika princess, Vasavi, who, after killing his father, usurped the throne of Magadha. Eventually, the Lichhavis supported a revolt against Ajatashatru by his younger stepbrother and the governor of Anga, Vehalla, who was the son of Bimbisara from his other Licchavika wife, Chellana, daughter of King Chetaka, who was the head of both the Licchavi republic and the Vajjika league.

Bimbisara had chosen Vehalla as his successor after a fallout with Ajatashatru, who had been caught conspiring against him. The Licchavikas had attempted to place Vehalla on the throne of Magadha after Ajatashatru's capture of the throne and had allowed Vehalla to use their capital, Vaishali, as the base for his revolt. After the failure of his rebellion, Vehalla sought refuge in his grandfather's home in Vaishali, the capital of the Licchavis and the Vajji league, following which Ajatashatru repeatedly attempted to negotiate with the Licchavikas and Vajjikas. After Ajatashatru's repeated negotiation attempts failed, he declared war on the Vajjika league in 484 BCE and conquered them in 468 BCE.

Ajatashatru practised an expansionist policy and defeated his neighbours, including the king of Kosala. His brothers, who equally claimed the Magadha throne, took refuge in Kashi, the capital of Kosala. It led to a war between Magadha and Kosala.

Ajatashatru conquered Kashi and captured the other smaller kingdoms in the Gangetic plains. Magadha, under Ajatashatru, became the most powerful kingdom in North India. He was a strategist and an innovator of new weapons and is credited with the invention of the *rathamusala* (scythed chariot) and the *mahashilakantaka* (engine to eject large stones).

The Buddha at Rajagriha

Rajagriha occupied a special place in the Buddha's heart. After leaving his father's palace in Kapilvastu, he first visited Vaishali and then Rajagriha. He spent time in solitude in the Pandava hills of Rajgir and later begged for alms in its streets, attracting many with his calm demeanour. Here, he met his five ascetic companions, who later received the first Dhamma sermon by the Buddha at Sarnath after his enlightenment.

When King Bimbisara came across Siddhartha Gautama seeking alms in the streets of Rajagriha, impressed by his aura and calm demeanour he entreated him to come and stay at his royal palace. However, the Buddha politely refused to go and stay at the palace. After his enlightenment at Bodh Gaya and the first turning of the wheel at Sarnath, he returned to Rajagriha, where he was given a grand welcome by the King Bimbisara himself at the city gates. He presented Venuvana, the royal bamboo grove to the Buddha, which became his residence in Rajagriha.

The adoption of Buddhism by King Bimbisara and his wife Khema was a great milestone in the history of Buddhism. Magadha was a rising power. They became the royal patrons of the Buddha and his teachings. King Bimbisara built a causeway leading up to the Vulture Peak (Griddhakuta Parvat). At the foot of the peak was Amaravana, the mango grove, offered to the

Buddha by the physician Jivaka. The remains of what was once a Jivakarama monastery can still be seen there.

Bimbisara's son Ajatashatru came to the Buddha to confess imprisoning and killing his own father. The Buddha enlightened him with his words, which are recorded in the *Sutra Dispelling the Regret of Ajatashatru*. He also sent his minister Vassakara to the Vulture Peak, where the Buddha was residing, to announce to him his plans to invade the Vajjika league and seek the Buddha's opinion on the matter. The Buddha, however, speaking to his disciple Ananda, laid down seven conditions that, if followed by the Vajjis, would not lead to their decline. Hearing it, Minister Vassakara said,

> If the Vajjis, Venerable Gotama, were endowed with only one or another of these conditions leading to welfare, their growth would have to be expected, not their decline. What then of all the seven? No harm, indeed, can be done to the Vajjis in battle by Magadha's king, Ajatasattu, except through treachery or discord. Well, then, Venerable Gotama, we will take our leave, for we have much to perform, much work to do.[1]

The final journey of the Buddha's life, which ended with the Mahaparinirvana at Kushinagar, began at Rajagriha. Shortly after this, the First Council—an assembly of 500 monks presided over by Mahakasyapa—met under the patronage of Ajatashatru in the Sataparna Cave, which was located southwest of Venuvana, and compiled the Buddha's teachings into a collection known as the *Sthaviranikaya*. Ashoka later erected a stupa in honour of the First Council at the place to the west of Sataparna Cave where at the same time, the *mahasanghikas*, regarded by some as proto-mahayanists, compiled their canon.

When Xuanzang visited Rajagriha, he came across a monastery and the Karanda Pond, where the Buddha used to bathe—a site that exists today within Venuvana. King Ajatashatru built two stupas, one over a portion of the the Buddha's relics and the other over his disciple Ananda's relics. Later, Ashoka unearthed the first of the two stupas to obtain relics for his 84,000 stupas.

The sites of many of these events may still be found in and around Rajgir, which is also a flourishing pilgrimage centre of the Hindus, Buddhists and Jains. There is also a Japanese temple near the remains of Ajatashatru's stupa.

Spiritual Rebirth of Shariputra and Maudgalyayana

The most important event during the Buddha's first visit to Rajagriha after his enlightenment was meeting Shariputra and Maudgalyayana, who became his two chief male disciples. Both hailed from Nalanda.

Legend has it that Shariputra met Ashvajit, last of the five ascetics to be influenced by the Buddha, while he was making his alms round one morning. He was greatly impressed by the monk's noble and calm demeanour and asked him what teachings he followed. He soon became an *arhant* (liberated) when he heard the Buddha's teachings from Ashvajit. He narrated what he had heard from Ashvajit to his childhood friend Maudgalyayana, who too became an arhant.

The two left their teacher, Sanjaya Belatthiputra, and came with five hundred of his followers to meet the Buddha at Venuvana. The Buddha welcomed them all and accepted Shariputra, possessing greater intelligence, and Maudgalyayana, wielding great miraculous powers, as his chief disciples.

Shariputra's preeminent role in comprehending and preaching the Dharma is evident in many early Buddhist texts. In a Pali sutta, a monk named Vangisa composed the following verses, praising his skill in Buddhist teaching:

> Deep in wisdom, intelligent,
> expert in the variety of paths;
> Shariputra, so greatly wise,
> teaches Dhamma to the mendicants.
> He teaches in brief,
> or he speaks at length.
>
> His call, like a myna bird,
> overflows with inspiration.
>
> While he teaches
> the mendicants listen to his sweet voice,
> sounding attractive,
> clear and graceful.
>
> They listen joyfully,
> their hearts elated.[2]

The Second Turning of the Wheel of Dharma at Rajagriha

The Buddha's most important association with Rajagriha is with Griddhakuta Parvat. The sacredness of a cave on it can well be understood by the fact that it might be the only surviving structure (naturally intact) where the Buddha set forth the second turning of the wheel of Dharma to an assembly of 5,000 monks, nuns and laity, as well as innumerable bodhisattvas after sixteen years of his enlightenment. His collection of teachings, which extended over twelve years, includes the *Saddharmapundarika Sutra* or Lotus Sutra and the *Surangama Samadhi Sutra*, as well as many *Prajnaparamita Sutras,* which contain the very essence of all his teachings.

The Chinese pilgrim Faxian mentions a cave at the Vulture Peak and Xuanzang a hall slightly below it, where the Buddha is said to have sat and preached. According to Xuanzang, once a monastery was there on Vulture Peak, inhabited by arhants and monks.

The Ratna Hill above the Vulture Peak is now crowned by Vishwa-Shanti Stupa, built recently by Japanese Buddhists. In a nearby temple, the sound of Japanese drums and Buddhist chants can be heard.

Shariputra and the *Heart Sutra*

Rajagriha's Vulture Peak connection to Mahayana teachings on Shunyata (emptiness) and the *Prajnaparamita Sutras* makes it special in the history and philosophical development of Buddhism, as well as its connection with Shariputra, who was born in Nalanda. Of all the *Prajnaparamita* literature, *Heart Sutra* contains the essence of the Buddha's teaching on emptiness. The Sutra begins by establishing the significance of the place

' Homage to Bhagavati Prajnaparamita!

Thus have I heard. At one time
the Blessed one was dwelling in
Rajgraha at Vulture Peak mountain,
together with a great community of
monks and a great
community of Boddhisatvas'[3]

'As with many sutras, the Buddha himself does not utter a word in the *Heart Sutra,* other than his confirmation at the end. Instead, he inspires a teaching to take place through the power of his meditation, and then gives his seal of approval, in this case to Avalokiteshavara, who has been expounding the words of the *Heart Sutra* to Shariputra.'[4]

Namah sarvajnaaya
Adoration to the All knowing!

Aaryaavalokiteshvara-bodhisattvo gambhiiraayaam prajnaapaaramitaayaam caryaam caramaano vyavalokayati sma: panca skandhaah; taamshca svabhaava-shuunyaan pashyati sma

Aarya-avalokiteshvara Bodhisattva performing the deep practice in the Perfection of Transcendent Wisdom, contemplated– finding all five aggregates empty in nature

Iha Shariputra ruupam shuunyataa shuunyataiva ruupam, ruupaam na prithak shuunyataa, shuunyataayaa na prithak ruupam, yad ruupam saa shuunyataa, yaa shuunyataa tad ruupam

Thus, Shariputra, form is emptiness and emptiness itself is form; emptiness is nothing but form, and form is nothing but emptiness; that which is form is emptiness, and that which is emptiness is form

Evem eva vedanaa-samjnaa-samskaara-vijnaanaani.
So are sensation, perception, volition and consciousness.

Iha Shariputra sarva-dharmaah shuunyataa-lakshanaa, anutpannaa, aniruddhaa, amalaa, na vimalaa, nonaa, na paripuurnaah.

Thus, Shariputra, all things have the character of emptiness; they are neither born nor cease; they are neither pure nor impure, neither incomplete nor complete.

Tasmaac Shariputra shuunyaayaam na ruupam na vedanaa na samjnaa na samskaaraa na vijnaanaani.

Therefore, Shariputra, the emptiness is formless, without sensation, perception, volition or consciousness

Na cakshuh-shrotra-ghraana-jihvaa-kaaya-manaamsi.
Without eye, ear, nose, tongue, body or mind

Na ruupa-shabda-gandha-rasa-sprashtavya-dharmaah
Without form, sound, smell, taste, touch or dharma

Na cakshurdhaatur yaavan na mano-vijnaana-dhaatuh
Without the realms of sight or consciousness.

Na vidyaa, naavidyaa, na vidyaa-kshayo, naavidyaa-kshayo, yaavan na jaraa-maranam na jaraamarana-kshayo, na duhkha-samudaya-nirodha-maargaa, na jnaanam, na praaptir apraaptitvena

Without wisdom, or ignorance, or extinction of wisdom or extinction of ignorance, etc., or old age and death or the extinction of old age and death, suffering or cause of suffering, extinction of suffering, or the path leading to extinction of suffering, without wisdom or acquisition or non-acquisition

Bodhisattvasya prajnaapaaramitaam aashritya viharaty acittaavaranah
Cittaavarana-naastitvaad atrasto, viparyaasaatikraanto nishtha-nirvaanah

Depending on the bodhisattva's Perfection of Transcendent Wisdom, one wanders without any mental barriers and

becomes fearless in their absence, thus freed from delusions,
attains Nirvana

Tryadhva-vyavasthitaah sarvabuddhaah prajnaapaaramitaam
aashrityaanuttaraam samyaksambodhim abhisambuddhaah
All Buddhas in all three realms attain complete enlightenment
through the Perfection of Transcendent Wisdom

Tasmaaj jnaatavyo prajnaapaaramitaa-mahaamantro
mahaavidyaa-mantro 'nuttara-mantro 'samasama-
mantrah, sarvadukha-prashamanah, satyam amithyatvaat,
prajnaapaaramitaayaam ukto mantrah
Therefore, the Great Mantra of the Perfection of Transcendent
Wisdom is the mantra of Great Wisdom, ultimate and
unparallel Mantra, extinguishing all suffering, is completely
true, nothing but true Mantra proclaimed in the Perfection of
Transcendent Wisdom

Tad yathaa gate gate paaragate paarasamgate bodhi svaaha
Thus, gone, gone, gone beyond;
gone completely beyond. Enlightened.

Iti prajnaapaaramitaa-hridayam samaaptam.
Thus ends the Heart of the Transcendent Wisdom Sutra.

Later, Shariputra's birthplace, Nalanda, gradually became the
centre of Mahayana Buddhism and the teaching of the philosophy
of Shunyata. German philosopher Arthur Schopenhauer, in
the final words of his main work, compared his doctrine to the
Shunyata of the *Heart Sutra*. Schopenhauer wrote: '...to those in
whom the will [to continue living] has turned and has denied
itself, this very real world of ours, with all its Suns and Milky

Ways, is — nothing.'[5] To this, he appended the following note: 'This is also the Prajna–Paramita of the Buddhists, the 'beyond all knowledge,' in other words, the point where subject and object no longer exist.'[6]

Xuanzang recalls that he travelled about 15 kilometers, from Rajagriha to Nalanda. He writes that, in a former life, the Buddha was a ruler of the kingdom in Nalanda, and because of his compassion for living beings and delight in almsgiving, people called him Shi Wu Yan—The Insatiable in Almsgiving, which is the source of the Tang Chinese name for Nalanda (Shiwuyan). He further adds that the land on which Nalanda was built was a mango grove in the centre of which was a pool that was home to a serpent (Naga) named Nalanda, the origin of the monastery's name. Some 500 merchants purchased this mango grove, he reports, with 10 kotis (crores) of gold coins and gifted it to the Buddha, who, he says, preached here for three months. Later, King Sakraditya selected this sacred spot by divination and constructed the monastery on it. However, Sakraditya is generally taken to be Kumaragupta I (c. 415–455 CE), who ruled about a millennium after the time of the Buddha.[7]

Mahavira too achieved nirvana at Pawapuri, less than 20 kilometres from Nalanda where a new temple is located in the middle of a lake, but the remains of other Jain temples are in close proximity.

Nalanda: An Ancient Centre of Scholarly Debates

'A yojana southwest from this place [Rajgir] brought them to the village of Nala, where Shariputra was born, and to which also he returned, and attained here his parinirvana. Over the spot (where his body was burned) there was a tope, which is still in existence.' –Faxian

The emergence of States (1400 BCE–600 BCE) in the Gangetic plains in the post Vedic period brought stability, prosperity and improved security to the society, creating space for leisure, creativity and curiosity, setting in motion a culture of debate and discussion that gave birth to an argumentative society, which possessed the tools to win an argument such as logic, justification and proof-building. These contributed in developing Indian logic and philosophy.

As many as sixty-three sects, including the Nigantha, emerged with a primary focus on asserting their intellectual and philosophical superiority.

Royal courts organized regular scholarly debates and disputations where the rival groups competed against each other for supremacy. On these occasions, the top scholars of their respective sects or schools tried to establish their supremacy by proving their opponents' inferiority in knowledge. It was a way to acquire patronage, recognition and to increase the number of followers for their sects and schools.

Nalanda was such a centre of learning and debate for the scholars before it became a Buddhist centre of knowledge where the recursive argument method was used to win scholarly debates. Lama Lozang Jamspal, describing the glory of Nalanda as the greatest Buddhist centre in Magadha in his work *Nalanda: A Stronghold of Scholarly Debates*, highlights Nalanda as the birthplace of Shariputra and Maudgalyayana and their legends from the *Sarvastinvadin Vinaya* texts of the Buddhist canon. A legend from *Vinayavastu* sheds light on Nalanda and the ancient tradition of scholarly debates:

In South India, there lived a learned scholar well-versed in the Vedas and Vedangas. He had students from all over the country. His students asked him one day if there were any other learned scholars like their teacher anywhere. The teacher replied that Magadha has even greater scholars than him.

So, they decided to go to Magadha along with their teacher. They were received respectfully at Rajagriha. As courtesy demanded, he went to see King Bimbisara and told him that he wanted to debate with the learned scholars of his kingdom. The king asked his ministers to find the greatest scholar in the Vedas from his kingdom. They proposed the name of Vasalaputra, learned in the Vedas and Vedangas, who lived in Nalanda.

Vasalaputra was invited to debate with the scholar from the South. The king ordered the ministers to prepare a stage for the debate. A teacher from the South as a guest was invited to lead the debate. Vasalaputra won the debate.

Commending Vasalaputra, the king announced to the public that the revenues of Nalanda would henceforth be given to Vasalaputra as a reward for winning the scholarly debate.

He had a son who was named Dirghordhvakaya. He grew into an accomplished man, well versed in the four Vedas and capable of expressing his views with clarity. Later, they had a daughter whom they named Sarika as her eyes were like those of the *Sarika* (Maina bird). She often engaged in scholarly debates with her brother Dirghordhvakaya and defeated him. This got his father worried, wondering who would safeguard the revenues of Nalanda after his death.

Later, a scholar named Tisya, adept in the Vedas and Vedangas and a specialist in Lokayata[8] philosophy, visited King Bimbisara and expressed his desire to have a scholarly debate with the most learned scholar of Magadha. Vasalaputra was again called upon from Nalanda. Tisya won the debate.

The king had to now reward Tisya. The ministers advised the king to hand over the revenue of Nalanda and institutionalize the practice of giving its revenue to the winner of scholarly debates in Magadha. The king agreed to this. The revenue of Nalanda was taken from Vasalaputra and given to Tisya. Vasalaputra was sad and started preparing to go into exile.

Tisya did not want Vasalaputra and his family to leave Nalanda and offered to share the revenue of Nalanda with them. Vasalaputra thought that Tisya would be a suitable match for his daughter Sarika and shared his thoughts with his wife, who readily agreed. However, his son Dirghordhvakaya did not approve of it. He said that Tisya is an opponent and will destroy them all in the end.

However, they did not pay heed to their son's remarks and married off their daughter, Sarika, to Tisya. Dirghordhvakaya thought he was humiliated by his parents because he didn't have enough education. Since Tisya knew Lokayata, he should also learn it and left for South India to study Lokayata philosophy.

Sarika gave birth to a boy who was named Upatishya after his father. Tisya, however, wanted him to be named after his mother. So, he named the boy Shariputra.

Under the guidance of his father, Shariputra became an expert in the four Vedas, Vedangas, and Indravyakarana. At the age of sixteen, he defeated all his opponents in scholarly debates. This event is recorded in *Karmasataksutra*[9].

Thus, Nalanda became the ancient economic, intellectual and philosophical centre of India, which created the conditions for establishing Nalanda Mahavihara by institutionalizing the tradition of scholarly debates and discussions, which was an essential part of its culture.

2

Nalanda's Legendary Sons: Shariputra and Maudgalyayana

I was in Patna at the end of February 2024 and wanted to call on the Governor of Bihar. However, I was informed that he was in Thailand, heading a twenty-two-member delegation along with the Union Minister of Social Justice and Empowerment, accompanying the four Holy Piparahwa Relics of Lord Buddha and his two Chief Disciples, Arahata Shariputra and Arahata Maudgalyayana, for a 26-day exposition. The delegation consisted of venerable monks from Kushinagar, Aurangabad and Ladakh; officials from the Ministry of Culture, the state government of MP, curators from the National Museum, artists and scholars. The event was organized with the support of the Ministry of External Affairs, the International Buddhist Confederation, New Delhi, the National Museum of India and the State Government of Madhya Pradesh.

The Holy Relics had left India from Delhi with the delegation, after customary ceremonies. These relics of Lord Buddha belonged to twenty of the special relics kept in the National Museum of India. Four of these were taken to Thailand for this momentous occasion. Additionally, the Holy Relics of two esteemed disciples of Lord Buddha, Arhant Shariputra and Arhant Maudgalyayana, currently housed at Sanchi, were also taken to Thailand and showcased together for the first time. The relics were carried in Indian Air Force aircraft befitting their status as State guests.

The Holy Relics were received with great reverence and ceremony at the Bangkok Military Airport by the Minister of Culture, Royal Thai Government, Thai officials and a large number of monks, among other dignitaries, were welcomed with an auspicious chanting ceremony and warm hospitality. The Minister of Culture of Thailand and Thai officials, along with the Indian Union Minister and delegates, then carried the Holy Relics from the Military Airport to the National Museum of Bangkok for safekeeping and later to be enshrined in a grand mandapam prepared in Sanam Luang Pavilion in Bangkok.

The Union Minister of Social Justice of the Government of India and the Minister of Culture of Thailand held a press conference at the National Museum, Bangkok on the arrival of the Holy Relics. Addressing the media, the Union Minister of India said the eternal message of Lord Buddha embodied in the great religion of Buddhism is the most important and unbreakable link between India and Thailand. He expressed hope that as they embarked on a new and more glorious chapter in bilateral relations between India and Thailand, the arrival of the Holy Relics would further strengthen the bond of friendship and love between the two countries. The Thai Culture Minister expressed joy and gratitude with the Government of India, having accepted the request of the Thai Government to send Holy Relics to Thailand for exposition.

The exhibition itinerary included multiple venues across Thailand, allowing devotees and enthusiasts alike to pay homage to these revered relics in Sanam Luang Pavilion, Bangkok, Ho Kum Luang, Royal Rujapruek, Chiang Mai, Wat Maha Wanaram, Ubon Ratchathani and Wat MahaThat, Aoluek in Krabi. The Holy Relics were escorted back on 19 March 2024 from Thailand to their respective homes, concluding a historic and spiritually enriching exposition in Thailand.

Such reverence for the Buddha and his two chief disciples—Shariputra and Maudgalyayana—filled me with great curiosity and wonder to explore more deeply about their lives, who are so highly revered beyond the Indian borders.

Xuanzang noted during his visit to Nalanda in the seventh century CE that Kolita, better known as Maudgalyayana, was born about 3 kilometers southwest of Nalanda at Kulika village, which is considered to be the present Jagdishpur, where a huge stone-seated black Buddha statue still exists.

Upatiṣya, better known as Shariputra, was born on the same day as Kolita. They were childhood friends. Upatiṣya and Kolita both became masters of the Vedas through their education, and each had a large number of young followers. One day, the two friends, during a festival in Rajagriha, were overcome by the realization that life is impermanent, and they felt a sense of spiritual urgency.

Realizing the futility of the impermanent material world, the two friends set out as ascetics in search of the path to end the cycle of birth, death and rebirth. As per *Mulasarvastivada* texts, both explored all six major ideologues active at Rajagriha at that time but concluded that none could lead them to nirvana. According to Pali texts, both studied under the guidance of Sanjaya Belatthiputra, a teacher of dialectical existentialism as per the Pali texts. Shariputra and Maudgalayayana eventually became dissatisfied with his teachings and left. They went their separate ways in search of truth, promising to inform each other if any one of them found the true path to nirvana.

One day, Shariputra saw the monk Asvajit, one of the Buddha's first five arhant disciples, teaching in the city of Rajagriha. Shariputra was impressed with the calm and serenity on his face and wanted to know more about him. Asvajit uttered these words . . .

Ye Dharma Hetu[1]...
All that arise from a cause,
Tathagata has explained their cause;
And their end,
Thus has spoken the Great Sage.

Hearing these words, Shariputra attained *sotapanna*, the first stage of enlightenment. He then went to Maudgalyayana and narrated the whole incident to him. After hearing these words, he also attained *sotapanna*. That day, a large number of Sanjaya Belatthiputra's disciples left him and went to seek spiritual guidance from the Buddha. They were all ordained as monks under the Buddha and became enlightened arhants.

After Shariputra and Maudgalyayana were ordained, the Buddha declared them his two chief disciples (*agrashavaka*). This was as per the past practice of appointing a pair of chief disciples by the former Buddhas, according to the Buddhist belief. It is believed that Maudgalyayana attained *arhatship* one week after being ordained, following intense meditation training while Shariputra attained arhatship two weeks after being ordained when he was fanning the Buddha. Shariputra required longer training and preparation to discharge his duties as Budha's first chief disciple.

Shariputra and Maudgalyayana are together referred to as 'the chief pair of disciples, the excellent pair' in the *Mahapadana Sutta*. As per the *Mahavagga*,[2] the Buddha declared them his two chief male disciples for being foremost in wisdom and in psychic powers. The texts describe that none of the Buddha's other disciples could answer questions that Maudgalyayana could, while Maudgalyayana was unable to answer questions which Shariputra could. Shariputra, being the first chief disciple, customarily sat to the Buddha's right, while Maudgalyayana, the second chief disciple sat to the left. They are, therefore, regarded as the right hand and left hand of the Buddha.

Shariputra's role was to organize the Buddha's teachings systematically as the first chief disciple. He put queries to the Buddha and entreated him to answer and himself clarified points and questioned other fellow disciples to test their knowledge. Shariputra elaborated and delivered sermons on topics proposed by the Buddha. He often asked Shariputra to teach in his place while he rested. His mastery in teaching the Dharma earned him the honorific *Dharmasenapati*.

The Sangha was led by Shariputra, who routinely took on the Buddha's role in managing its affairs. This included ordaining new monks, planning their travels and other responsibilities. The Buddha entrusted him to ordain his son Rahula.

He was also entrusted to conduct scholarly debates with the teachers of other faiths and philosophies who challenged the Buddha. As per Mulasarvastivada texts, when a rift was created by Devadutta in the Buddha's Sangha, wherein he divided the monks and took some of them to another teacher, Shariputra restored the Sangha by winning them back with the superior power of his arguments. This account is considered to be historically authentic by André Bareau.[3] It is further supported by the accounts of the Chinese pilgrim Xuanzang who came across Devadatta's sect during his visit to India that had continued to flourish.

As per the extant Buddhist texts, Shariputra is generally credited with the establishment of the monastic rules after exhorting the Buddha to create them. He was known for his strict adherence to them.

Shariputra achieved *Parinirvana* in Nalanda shortly before the *Mahaparinirvana* of the Buddha. After having sensed that his end was nearing, he travelled to Nalanda to bring his mother Sarika into the fold of Buddhism. Afterwards, on the full moon day of Kartika, he passed away peacefully.

His remains were cremated at Rajagriha and a funeral was held there. Cunda, the younger brother of Shariputra brought his relics to the Buddha in Shravasti where he enshrined them at a chaitya in Jetavana.

Maudgalyayana

As mentioned earlier, Maudgalyayana was born near Nalanda in the village of Kulika. He was named after his mother. His father was the village chief. He was born on the same day as Shariputra. They became friends from childhood and later achieved enlightenment together. Considering their childhood bonds and organizational abilities and skills, the Buddha designated them as his two chief disciples.

Maudgalyayana was a popular teacher, and his sermons about afterlife destinations were very well received as per the *Mulasarvastivada Vinaya* and the *Divyavadana*. To honour Maudgalyayana, the Buddha instructed that an image depicting *Bhavachakra*, the Wheel of Becoming, portraying different realms of the cycle of existence, the three poisons in the mind (greed, hatred and delusion), and the teachings of *Pratityasamutpada* (dependent origination), be painted at the gate of Venuvana in Rajagriha and the law of karma be explained to all the visitors. Images of the Wheel of Becoming are found across Buddhist Asia.

Maudgalyayana is considered the one who created the first the Buddha image, the Udayana Buddha. The image was said to depict all the thirty-two signs of a Buddha.

He is mentioned in the *Ullambana Sutra*, which covers atoning for the sins of ancestors. Ullambana is the foundation for the popular Japanese tradition of Obon, which deals with ancestor worship.

It is believed that the day Maudgalyayana performed the act of compassionate ancestors' worship and brought salvation to his forefathers, it was celebrated as Ullambana, which falls in the middle of the seventh Buddhist lunar month, more popularly known as the Buddha's Joyful Day or Sangha Day. Prayers are offered on this day to the departed ancestors and to living parents and elders.

On *Magha Puja* in Sri Lanka, which is better known as *Navam Full Moon Poya*, Maudgalyayana's appointment as the chief disciple of the Buddha is celebrated.

Maudgalyayana is considered to be the author of several verses in the *Theragatha* and many *sutras* in the *Samyutta Nikaya*. His knowledge of ethics, philosophy and meditation is thought to be exemplary. The Dharmaguptaka school, one of the early Buddhist schools, finds its origin in Maudgalyayana.

It is believed that Maudgalyayana was killed by robbers hired by a rival sect at a cave in Udayagiri hills at Rajagriha shortly after the Mahaparinirvana of the Buddha according to the Pali texts.

Holy Relics of Shariputra and Maudgalyayana

The holy relics of Shariputra and Maudgalyayana were accidentally discovered in 1851 by archaeologists Alexander Cunningham and Lieutenant Fred. C. Maisey during an excavation of one of the stupas in Sanchi. They found a pair of sandstone boxes with encased bone fragments inside them. Shariputra's and Maudgalyayana's names were inscribed on them in the Brahmi script. Shariputra's casket contained pieces of sandalwood believed to be part of his funeral pyre. Another pair of boxes with encased bone fragments of Shariputra and Maudgalyayana was found at the nearby town of Satdhara during another excavation of a stupa by Cunningham and Maisey.

Cunningham and Maisey divided the holy relics of Shariputra and Maudgalyayana among themselves. Maisey brought the Satdhara relics to Britain and lent them to the Victoria and Albert Museum in London in 1866, which were eventually sold to the Museum in 1921 by Maisey's son. Cunningham brought his share of the holy relics from Sanchi to Britain on two ships, one of which sank.

Buddhist organizations in India and Myanmar started putting pressure on the British government in the early twentieth century to return the holy relics of Shariputra and Maudgalyayana to India. The British government eventually asked the Victoria and Albert Museum to return the relics for diplomatic reasons, despite its resistance. However, they decided to return the relics to Sri Lanka and not to India. In accordance with an agreement made with Buddhist organizations, the relics were temporarily displayed at the Colombo Museum in 1947 before being sent to India in 1949. A tour was organized for the holy relics to be displayed at prominent Buddhist locations in north India.

In 1950, Burmese Prime Minister U Nu later asked India for a portion of these relics. In 1952, the erstwhile Indian prime minister Jawaharlal Nehru decided to make a 'permanent loan' of a portion of the relics to Burma where they were enshrined in the Kaba Aye Pagoda. The same year, a portion of the relics was also given to Sri Lanka, which is kept at the Maha Bodhi Society in Sri Lanka. The Indian portion of the holy shrine was enshrined at the Chethiyagiri Vihara in Sanchi in 1952, which was recently taken to Thailand for veneration as narrated above.

3

The Rise of Nalanda Mahavihara

Nalanda is located on a slightly raised landscape in the Gangetic plains with abundant water bodies. It has been a sacred place for the Jains, Ajivikas, Buddhists and Hindus since ancient times.

Shariputra was born in the vicinity of Nalanda and attained his parinirvana there. Emperor Ashoka constructed a stupa at Nalanda in the third century BCE, which became the nucleus of the Nalanda Mahavihara. [1]

As per Hwui Li, the biographer of the Chinese pilgrim Xuanzang who visited Nalanda Mahavihara in the seventh century CE— 'the land on which Nalanda was built was previously a mango grove with a pond. A serpent resided in this pond known as Nalanda, which eventually lent its name to the monastery. Another narrative is derived from the Jataka tales wherein the Buddha, in one of his past lives, reigned as a compassionate king at the site of Nalanda. Renowned for his immense generosity, the king was called 'the Insatiable Almsgiver,' which inspired the Tang Chinese name for Nalanda-*Shiwuyan*.[2]'

The seeds of the Nalanda Mahavihara were sown in the backdrop of the revival of Buddhism in Magadha when Emperor Ashoka adopted Buddhism after the bloody Kalinga war and built a stupa in Nalanda in the 3rd C BCE. It is recorded that the emperor also established a vihara or 'college' along with the stupa, which, received the support of the wealthy local merchants (*shresthis*) like Suvishnu. Monk scholars taught Buddhist *abhidhamma* at the Vihara and gradually its reputation grew with the passage of time, and it evolved into Nalanda Mahavihara. While visiting the Mahavihara, Xuanzang observed:

> '...the whole establishment is surrounded by a brick wall, which encloses the whole convent from without. One gate opens into the great college, from which are separated eight other halls, standing in the middle (of the Sangharama). The richly adorned towers, and the fairy-like turrets, like pointed hill-tops, are congregated together. The observatories seem to be lost in the vapours (of the morning), and upper rooms tower over the clouds. From the windows one may see how the winds and the clouds (produce new forms), and above the soaring eaves the conjunctions of the sun and moon may be observed. And then we may add how the deep, translucent ponds, bear on their surface the blue lotus, intermingled with Kie-ni (Kanaka[3]) flower of deep red colour, and at intervals the Amra groves spread all over their shade.'

This observation of Xuanzang is corroborated by the Baragaon (Nalanda) Stone Inscription of Yasovarman of the eighth century CE—

> 'Bālāditya, the great king of irresistible valour, after having vanquished all the foes and enjoyed the entire earth, erected as if with a view to see the Kailāsa mountain surpassed, a great and extraordinary temple (prāsāda) of the illustrious son of

Śuddhodana (i.e. the Buddha) here at Nālandā. Nālandā had scholars, well-known for their (knowledge of the) sacred texts and arts, and (was full of the) beams of the rays of the chaityas shining and bright like white clouds. She was (consequently) mocking, as it were, at all the cities of the kings who had acquired wealth by tearing asunder the temples of the great elephants surrounded by the shining black bees which were maddened by drinking the rut in hostile lands. She had a row of vihāras, the line of whose tops touched the clouds. That (row of vihāras) was, so to say, the beautiful festoon of the earth, made by the Creator, which looked resplendent in going upwards. Nālandā had temples which were brilliant on account of the network of the rays of various jewels set in them and was the pleasant abode of the learned and virtuous Saṃgha and resembled Sumeru, the charming residence of the noble Vidyādharas. (The prāsāda) stands aloft, as if it were a column of the great fame it had won, scoffing at the lustre of the moon, disregarding the beauty of the summits of the Snow-mountains (Himālaya), soiling (i.e. throwing into the shade) the white Ganges of the sky, and then turning dumb the streams of disputants...As long as the moon shines and the sun, lamp of the world...so long let this glory (kīrti), which is pure like the moon (candra), whiten the circle of (all) the quarters.[4]

The massive external grandeur of the buildings contrasted with the delicate artistic beauty of their interior. 'All the outside courts, in which are the priests' chambers, are of four stages. The stages have dragon projections, and coloured eaves, pearl-red pillars, carved and ornamented, richly adorned balustrades, while the roofs are covered with tiles that reflect the light in a thousand shades. These things add to the beauty of the scene. The Sangharamas of India are counted by myriads, but this is the most remarkable in grandeur and height.'[5] Xuanzang also remarks; 'In this establishment, the work of a succession of sovereigns, the sculpture was perfect and really beautiful'. He also saw an image of the Buddha in the Sakraditya monastery. Yijing saw eight halls and three hundred apartments in the whole monastery.

Xuanzang writes that a king named Sakraditya selected the site and built a Vihara on it. Then his successor and son Buddhagupta built another monastery to the south of the original one, while Tathagatagupta built one to the east and finally King Baladitya built a fourth monastery to the northeast. The Spanish Jesuit priest H. Heras has identified the above four kings as Kumaragupta I, Skandagupta, Purnagupta, and Narshimhagupta respectively. [6]

The third and last phase of the expansion of Nalanda Mahavihara took place between the mid-eighth and twelfth centuries during the Pala Dynasty, until its decline and complete abandonment in the fourteenth century.

Discovery and Excavation of the Archaeological Remains of Nalanda

Nalanda Mahavihara had completely disappeared from the public consciousness in India between the fifteenth and eighteenth centuries. Francis Buchanan-Hamilton explored the site of Baragaon in the vicinity of Nalanda in 1811–12 and found some Hindu and Buddhist statues. Markham Kittoe established the connection between the site and the ruins of the Nalanda Mahavihara in 1847. In 1853, the French sinologist Stanislas Julien, well versed in Sanskrit and Mandarin, published a French translation of Xuanzang's *The Tang Record on the Western Regions*, which had a detailed description of his travels in India during the seventh century CE. Its publication in France was a landmark event that ignited the imagination of scholars specializing in exploring

India's history, particularly British explorers such as Alexander Cunnigham, who tried to identify the sites visited by Xuanzang.

Accurate descriptions of Xuanzang helped the archaeologists to identify Nalanda Mahavihara's archaeological site in the nineteenth century CE, which was later confirmed by the inscriptions found on seals at Nalanda. The actual name of the monastery *Srī-Nālandā-Mahāvihārīyāryabhikṣusaṃghasya* or 'of the noble monastic community of the Great Monastery of Nalanda' is found in an 8th century terracotta seal inscription unearthed during the excavations at Nalanda.

Alexander Cunnigham conducted archaeological inquiries in 1862–63, which were published in 1871. He saw rows of massive conical-shaped mounds, which he thought were the lofty temples of Nalanda Mahavihara.

On October 15, 1872, A M Broadley, the Deputy Magistrate of Bihar district set out to excavate the 'great central tumulus' at Nalanda, a place he described as 'the monastery, or, more strictly and correctly speaking, the university of Nalanda', being perhaps the first to describe the institution as a university.

The first systematic excavation at Nalanda was conducted by the Archaeological Survey of India (ASI) from 1915–1937, and the second one from 1974–82. A great stupa, five chaityas (temples) and eleven viharas (monasteries) and innumerable votive stupas and shrines were found during the excavations. Monasteries were located in a row westward, facing the temple, which was in the east facing the monasteries. The Great Stupa, or the Great Monument of Site 3, at the southern end of the monastery in the temple row was a stupa encased in a temple (*stupa-chaitya*), made of brick like the other monasteries and temples at Nalanda and adorned with stucco dating from the seventh century. A small shrine was located at the top of it, which is accessible by a makeshift staircase.

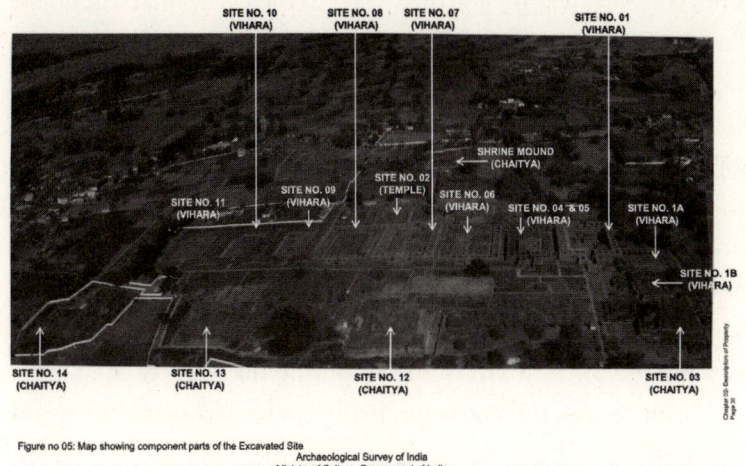

Figure no 05: Map showing component parts of the Excavated Site
Archaeological Survey of India
Ministry of Culture, Government of India

Layout

'The excavated remains of Nalanda are located atop an elevated (300 meters) plane, aligned in an approximately north–south direction, tilting slightly towards east. This slightly elevated landform is located in an otherwise flat land, drained by a palaeo-channel of the Ganges. The drying of the channel led to the formation of a fertile (plain) with water bodies (left behind after drying) and covered by a wooded area. (While) habitation patterns changed the original landscape by thinning forest cover, reducing the number of water bodies and flattening(flatting) much of the land, the elevated land atop which the Mahavihara was laid out is evident till date.'[7]

However, the boundary wall or the famous gates of Nalanda Mahavihara, where the visitors were tested by the *Dvarpala Pandita*, are yet to be located. 'The mound in Begumpur, 2 km north of the excavated site, referred to as the mud-fort of Khamgar Khan, is at times considered as the northern gate to the Mahavihara. Scholars like Dr Stewart mention that the main gate to the university was in the south, and within it was a large well (Loizzo)—none of which has however been identified (Archaeological Survey of India, 1916–2001). Also, no remains of the famed library Dharmaganja have been found.'[8]

'The layout of Nalanda Mahavihara visible today after excavation of the southernmost cluster constituting viharas numbered 1 to 7 and chaityas numbered 1 to 4 was laid out between the 5th and 7th centuries during the reign of the Gupta rulers. Of course, there were periodic repairs, reconstructions and additions carried out over centuries to this basic layout, which were recorded in seals, inscriptions, and stone tablets that provide valuable information on the expansion of the Mahavihara. The temples were expanded, existing viharas were repaired, and new viharas numbered 9, 10, and 11 were constructed during the rule of Gopala, Mahipala, and Devapala of the Pala dynasty. During this period, a shrine was added to the central courtyard of Sites No.01, 04-05, 08 and 10. A shrine located to the east of Site No. 07 also belongs to this period.'[9]

The numerous votive stupas found at the Mahavihara commemorate the great scholars who dedicated their lives to the cause of the Mahavihara. Among these, the votive stupas made of stucco were constructed during the late Gupta period, while the stupas made of stone were constructed during the Pala period.

> 'The built ensembles show the conscious shift from a clustered layout to a linear alignment reflecting the design principle adopted to accommodate the changes in rituals and the growing scholarship. The oldest structures dateable between 3rd century BCE to 6th century CE constitute the Site No. 03 and Sites numbered 1A, 1B, 1 and unnamed structure north

of 1B which show a clustered formation, reminiscent of the layout evident in earlier educational facilities, like Takshashila '(Buddhist Ruins of Takht-i-Bahi and Neighboring City Remains at Sahr-i-Bahlol', WH Ref: 140), Pakistan. Excavation revealed layers of construction which indicate that the earlier viharas, especially 1A, 1B and 1 were located at a greater proximity to the sacred core i.e. the principal stupa.'[10]

'The later structures (built post 4th century CE) of Nalanda, in contrast, show a formal and physical segregation of secular and sacred functions. The north-south layout of the later Sites (04, 05, 06, 07, 08, 09, 10 and 11) and Sites (12, 13, 14 and Shrine Mound) follow the topographical features and has allowed for the systematic expansion of the Mahavihara unlike the clustered layout formed by the Site No. 03 and early viharas. The later (post 4th century CE) layout reflects a heightened emphasis on sacred structures where each chaitya was provided with an open space and were built in monumental scale.'[11]

Eleven viharas and three chaityas flank the eastern and western sides of the principal South-North axis emanating from the sacred centre of the Great stupa of Shariputra.

'In addition to these structures which depict an organized site-planning, are the remains of a temple till its plinth-level (Site No. 2), a fourth *chaitya* (referred to as Shrine Mound) located further east of the viharas and an unexcavated vihara to the north of Site No. 11.'[12]

'The alignment of mounds, presence of antiquities, the uniform shape of the water bodies and exploration of area beyond the excavated remains suggest Nalanda would have covered an area of at least 2 square kilometers and perhaps had two more columns of viharas apart from numerous *chaityas.*'[13]

Architecture

Buddhist chaityas are primarily of two forms—the panchayatan (quincuncial form) and the cruciform. A panchayatan chaitya consists of a quadrilateral base, which is a raised platform upon which the principal shrine is placed in the centre while on its four corners, subsidiary shrines are erected. The continuous path peripheral to the principal shrine and connecting the subsidiary shrines is called the *pradakshina patha* (circumambulation path).[14]

Over a period of seven centuries, the Great Stupa of Shariputra was transformed into a chaitya through seven successive phases of construction. This transition from stupa to chaitya to attain the final quincuncial form was adopted for all construction post sixth century CE. Of these, only rare examples of panchayatan chaityas have survived, which include the Mahabodhi temple and the Great Stupa at Nalanda. The latter retains the original brick and plaster construction of the fourth to eleventh centuries CE, as opposed to the Mahabodhi temple, which has largely been reconstructed.[15]

Patrons

Xuanzang mentions six monasteries built by six kings viz. Sakraditya, Vajra, Buddhagupta, Tathagatagupta, Baladitya and Harsha. King Harshavardhana of Kannauj is credited with the reconstruction of Nalanda by building a vihara and high boundary wall around the Mahavihara after its destruction by King Shashanka of Bengal. King Harshavardhana's seals were discovered during excavation indicating his provision of support for the monastery. Xuanzang notes, 'the king of the country (Harsha) remitted the revenues of about 100 villages for the endowment of the monastery'. Later, Yijing records, 'the lands in its possession bestowed upon the monastery by kings of many generations contained more than 200 villages'. A daily supply of a large quantity of rice, and also of butter and milk were contributed day by day by householders in these 200 villages.

After Harsha, Xuanzang mentions King Purnavarma, who 'presented to Nalanda a figure of the Buddha standing upright, and made of copper, 80 feet high', to cover which he also had a pavilion erected. It is assumed that Purnavarma might have been from the Maukhari dynasty, as suggested by H. Heras. One of the seals found at Nalanda mentions a king named Suresvaravarman and gives his genealogy. Further, an inscription states that Malada, a minister of King Yasovarmmadeva, offered various gifts to the monks of Nalanda, provided for their daily food and paid money which could buy the whole Vihara.

The kings of the Pala dynasty were great patrons of Nalanda. The name Dharmapala Deva occurs on a copper plate found at Nalanda bearing a defaced inscription. A number of metallic figures also refer to King Devapala. Then there are two inscriptions, one of which refers to the construction at Nalanda of a vihara by Balaputradeva, King of Suvarnadvipa (Sumatra), and the grant by King Devapaldeva of Bengal of five villages for the maintenance of this monastery at Balaputradeva's request conveyed to the Pala king by his Ambassador Balavarmman. The Ghosrawa inscription describes Devapala's favourite Viradeva, a Nalanda scholar who later became the Head of the Mahavihara.

King Gopala II is mentioned in an inscription on a statue of Goddess Vagisvari found at Nalanda. Kalyanamitra Chintamani references King Mahipala, son of Vigrahapala, noting that in the sixth year of his reign, he copied the valuable work *Ashtasahasrika Prajnaparamita*. The Gurjara–Pratihara King Mahendrapaladeva, who conquered Magadha around the tenth century CE is mentioned on a votive stupa at Nalanda.

Number of Students

Xuanzang tells his biographer Hwui Li—'The priests, belonging to the convent, or strangers (residing therein) always reach to the number 10,000...there are 1000 men who can explain 20 collections of Sutras and Shastras; 500 men who can explain 30 collections, and perhaps 10 men including the master of law who can explain 50 collections. Shilabhadra alone has studied and understood the whole number.'[16] Yijing records in his memoir that the number of monks staying at the monastery exceeded 3,000.

Commenting on the figures provided by Xuanzang and Yijing regarding the number of students at Nalanda Mahavihara, Frederick Asher writes:

'If the reports that there were 3000–10,000 monks at the monastery were accurate, Nalanda must have had a dynamic relationship with the surrounding agricultural region, and not just with the surrounding towns. It is undeniable that the surrounding region prospered substantially from the wealth of the monastery, however Nalanda in turn was also heavily dependent on goods and services from the surrounding region. Monasteries produce scholarship; however, they don't produce any goods or services other than ritual services but are rather exclusively consumers. Just to feed 3000 monks from Yijing's estimate, food alone would have been a huge enterprise. If each monk ate even half a kilogram of food per day, it would require 1.5 tons of food daily to feed 3000 monks. That is far more than the surrounding agricultural area could provide. However, we also need to think about the fact that the surrounding area and Magadha in general was a highly fertile region. These areas could produce as many as three crops per year, reducing the need to bring food from other faraway places.

In fact, one reason for the success of Nalanda monastery is attributed to the region's ability to supply large amounts of food to large, concentrated populations of monks. The area around the monastery was also known for having a number of lakes and water bodies.'[17]

Admission Process

Nalanda was famous for its specialization in the art of disputation and public speaking. Xuanzang writes, 'Foreign monks came to the establishment to put an end to their doubts and then became celebrated.' Indian and foreign monks from distant places like China, Korea, Tibet and Tokhara (Bactria) came to India to study at Nalanda, and to copy valuable Buddhist manuscripts. Fifty-six Chinese and Korean monks visited India; during the span of forty years between the visits of Xuanzang and Yijing, many of them visited Nalanda. As noted by Xuanzang, 'those who stole the name of Nalanda were all treated with respect wherever they went'.

The *dvarapandit* (Scholar at the gate) engaged in debates with the monks who wanted to study at Nalanda Mahavihara. A large number of them were turned back. 'The keeper of the gate poses some difficult questions; many are unable to answer and retire'[18] Xuanzang notes. He adds, 'Of those from abroad who wished to enter the schools of discussion the majority, beaten by the difficulties of the problems, withdrew; and those who were deeply versed in old and modern learning were admitted, only two or three out of ten succeeding.'[19]

According to Yijing, 'A student at 15 had to study *Vritti-sutra* which he finished at 20, after which he studied philosophy for two or three years at advanced institutions like Nalanda or Vallabhi.'[20] Thus, it can be said that the students seeking admission at Nalanda must have been in their twenties and above.

Intellectual Life

Xuanzang writes in his book *Tang Records of the Western Regions*:

> 'The priests, to the number of several thousands, are the men of highest ability and talent. Their distinction is great at the present time and there are many hundreds whose fame has rapidly spread through distant regions. Their conduct is pure and unblamable. They sincerely follow the precepts of moral law. The rules of the convent are severe, and all the priests are bound to observe them. The countries of India respect and follow them. The day is not sufficient for asking and answering profound questions. From morning till night they engage in discussion, the young and the old mutually help one another. Those who cannot discuss questions out of *Tripitaka* are little esteemed and are obliged to hide themselves for shame. Learned men from different cities, on this account, who desire to acquire quickly a renown in discussion, come here in multitudes to settle their doubts, and then the streams of their wisdom spread far and wide.'[21]

Several lectures and disputations went on simultaneously in the central courtyards of the monasteries and monks actively participated in them. Xuanzang tells his disciple Hwui Li, 'within the Temple, they arrange 100 pulpits for preaching, and the students attend these discourses without any fail, even for a minute.'

Diversity of Subjects Taught

The subjects taught at the Mahavihara covered a wide range of topics drawn from the different fields of learning. As Xuanzang notes, 'all study the Great Vehicle and the eighteen sects and not only so but even ordinary works such as Vedas and other books, the Hetuvidya, the Shabdavidya and the Chikitsavidya, the works of Magic (Atharvaveda), the Sankhya, besides these they thoroughly investigate the 'miscellaneous' works'.[22]

Xuanzang himself came to Nalanda to study Yogachara philosophy. He also studied other subjects like Nyaya, Hetuvidya, Shabdavidya and the Brahmanas, which covered wide areas of philology, law, philosophy, astronomy and the Sanskrit grammar of Panini.

Universalism and Freedom of Beliefs

Monks of all major and minor Buddhist sects, as well as non-Buddhists, came to study at Nalanda Mahavihara and engaged in debates and discussions as Xuanzang notes above. Nalanda became a peaceful battleground for various philosophical strands, ideas and thoughts, sects and creeds who engaged in arguments and scholarly debates. Despite acrimonious and animated debates and discussions, Nalanda never witnessed any violence among its monks. Xuanzang tells his disciple Hwui Li– 'The priests dwelling here, as a body, naturally (or spontaneously) are dignified and grave so that during the 700 years of the foundation of the establishment there has not been a single case of rebellion against the rules.'[23]

Intellectual and philosophical differences were a cause of celebration, and monks had the freedom of thought, expression and belief. The Mahavihara provided an atmosphere of freedom and tolerance where any dispute could be settled through debate, using the recursive argument method. This marked the first step in the process of scientific enquiry, laying the foundation of science in the 1st millennium CE. The winners in these debates were acclaimed universally.

Democratic Principles

Interestingly, Yijing, in his accounts, notes that rules and regulations governing life in the monasteries were stricter at Nalanda than elsewhere. The administration of the Mahavihara, which was the largest in the world, was done by the entire body of monks on democratic principles, including the annual assignment of rooms to monks, the trial and punishment of any offenses and the expulsion of those found guilty. Allocation of rooms was done on the basis of seniority. The new entrants and senior monks had harmonious relations among themselves, and any dispute was resolved through discussion, which became the Nalanda tradition of resolving conflicts.

Ranking of Monks

As per Xuanzang, the monks at Nalanda were ranked on the basis of the breadth of their knowledge of various disciplines rather than the depth of their knowledge of one particular subject. A monk's privileges depended on his rank. Strict protocol was followed for the head of the Mahavihara. Xuanzang wrote about his own reception at Nalanda and how he was presented before Silbhadra in his accounts.

Titles

Monks who took charge of the administration of the monastery had different academic titles such as Kulapati for the head of an institution as stated in a *Smriti* text:

> 'Muninam dasasahasram yonnadanena poshanat
> adhyapayati viprarshih asau kulapatih smritah.'

However, at Nalanda, the head of the Mahavihara was addressed as Pandita.

Allocation of Rooms

The monks were allocated rooms according to their seniority before the onset of the monsoon season, where the whole community of monks participated. As noted by Yijing, 'Rooms are assigned to each member; to the *Sthaviras* (elders), better rooms are given, and thus gradually to the youngest. In Nalanda, such rules are followed at present.'[24]

Yijiing noted the advantages of such democratic allocation of rooms at Nalanda Mahavihara: 'It removes one's selfish intention, and the rooms for monks are properly protected.'[25]

Time Keeping

Nalanda Mahavihara had the clepsydra, an ancient time-measuring device that functioned by a flow of water. The day was one of eight hours, each of which was indicated by four immersions of the smaller bowl in the larger vessel of water. Each such immersion was indicated by one strike of the drum, while the completion of one hour, as defined above, was announced by four strikes of a drum, two blasts of a conch-shell and an additional beat of the drum. The second hour ended at noon, when eating was prohibited. The afternoon, like the forenoon, consisted of two hours. The end of the first hour at night was announced by the beat of the drum by the *Karmadana*, the subdirector of the monastery himself. Sunrise and sunset were announced by the beat of a drum outside the gate of the monastery by 'the servants and porters' stationed there.[26]

Kitchen

'What we call a monastery,' says I-tsing, 'is a general designation for the place of residence (for the Sangha), the whole of which may be regarded as a monastic kitchen. In every apartment, raw and cooked food may be kept. (But), if sleeping in the monastery is not allowed, all the priests then residing must go out and lodge somewhere (else) . . . the keeping of provisions in a monastery is allowable (according to Vinaya) . . . the traditional custom of India is to consecrate the whole monastery as a "kitchen", but to take a part of it to be used as a kitchen is also allowed by the Buddha.'[27]

Bath

Xuanzang mentions the ponds of Nalanda in his accounts. Yijing writes— 'There are more than ten great pools near the Nalanda monastery, and there every morning a *ghanti* (gong) is sounded to remind the monks of the bathing hour. Everyone brings a bathing towel with him. Sometimes a hundred, sometimes a thousand monks leave the monastery together and proceed in all directions towards these pools, where all of them take a bath.' [28]

'Bathrooms were not provided, though for laundering clothes, an arrangement is seen at one place among the ruins where there is a set of cells with a central water reservoir and a stone slab at the opening of each cell for thrashing dirt out of wet clothes. Toilet arrangements also are conspicuous by their absence and the lack seems to suggest either that the Indian practice of defecation at a secluded spot out in the fields obtained or that there were trench lantrines now untraceable.'[29]

Library

During his stay at Nalanda, Xuanzang collected 657 sacred texts, while Yijing collected some 400 Sanskrit texts. Though no archaeological evidence has been found yet of the great library of Nalanda Mahavihara during excavations carried out so far, it becomes evident from the large number of Sanskrit texts collected by both Xuanzang and Yijing during their stay in Nalanda that there must have been a large repository of Sanskrit manuscripts at the Mahavihara with the facility and manpower to copy them.

As per the Tibetan accounts, Nalanda possessed a well-equipped library, which was known as the Dharmaganja, the 'Moutntain of Truth' which contained three divisions: *Ratnadadhi*, the 'Sea of Jewels', the Ratnasagara, the 'Ocean of Jewels', and the Ratnaranjaka, the 'Jewel-Adorned'. Ratnasagara was a nine-storey edifice. Its rich collection included rare sacred texts such as *Prajnaparamita-sutra* and Tantra books like *Samajaguhya*, among others.

Over centuries, Nalanda Mahavihara became a celebrated seat of learning, because of its historical, religious and philosophical importance, its proximity to power and its location in the fertile plains of Magadha.

4

The Luminaries of Nalanda

Nalanda nurtured a number of great scholars, philosophers, translators, poets, mathematicians, logicians, artisans, architects and astronomers, who immensely contributed to various fields, including Buddhist philosophy, Sanskrit grammar, language and literature which transformed the social, economic, political, religious and cultural landscape of Asia and the world

As per the accounts of Yijing—'The head of all the pandits, the teaching staff and others, was called a Superior. Under him was the Karmadana, or Viharaswami or Viharapala. He was the chief officer after the Superior and to him the utmost deference was paid.'[1]

Here is a brief introduction to some of these great luminaries of Nalanda:

Nagarjuna (c. first–third century CE) is considered the foremost thinker in the Mahayana tradition of Buddhism who advocated the Madhyamaka philosophy of Shunyata (emptiness). It is believed that he was born in the mid-first or early second century CE in South India in Vidarbha, once a kingdom, now a region in present-day Maharashtra and Andhra Pradesh. He studied at Nalanda, as per the Tibetan sources.

The two most important works of Nagarjuna which continue to be studied today are *Mulamadhyamakakarika* (Fundamental Verses on the Middle Path) and *Vigrahavyavartani* (The End of

Disputes). These works explore the nature of reality, our perception and the basis of knowledge.

In explaining Shunyata, Nagarjuna brings together key Buddhist doctrines, particularly *anatman* (non-self) and *pratityasamutpada* (dependent origination). For him, all phenomena (dhammas) are without any *svabhava* (own-being, self-nature, or inherent existence) and, thus, without any underlying essence. They are empty of inherent existence or of being independently existent. This is because all things come into existence dependently—not through their own power, but by relying on conditions that lead to their becoming, rather than simply being. He played a key role in the development of the two truths doctrine, that believes that there is the ultimate truth (*paramartha satya*) and the conventional truth (*saṃvṛtisatya*). The ultimate truth for him is Shunyata: the truth that everything is empty of essence.

Aryadeva (c. third century CE) is considered to be the most important philosopher in the Madhyamaka school of thought after Nagarjuna and was his disciple and godson. According to Karen Lang, Professor of Buddhist Studies at the University of Virginia, the earliest reference to Aryadeva is made by the famous translator Kumarjiva (c. 344–413 CE) in his work. The most important work of Aryadeva is *Catuḥsataka* (Four Hundred Verses), which is considered both to be a commentary on Nagarjuna's *Mulamadhyamakakarika* and a supplement to it. His *Sataka* and *Dvadasamukhasastra*, both translated by Kumarajiva in the fourth century, are important reference materials for the East Asian Madhyamaka school and are only available in Tibetan and Chinese translations. As per the legend, he debated with Matriceta, also known as Durdharsakala at Nalanda and defeated him. An account of this debate is included in the introduction to Aryadeva's *Catuhsataka*.

Asanga (c. fourth–fifth century CE) was the founder of the Yogachara school of thought and one of the most prominent figures in the history of Buddhism. His most important work is *Yogacharabhumi*. It is still widely studied in China, where it is known as *Yogacharabhumi Shastra*. It is believed that he was born in Purushapura (modern day Peshawar). His two most important works include *Mahayanasamgraha* (Summary of Mahayana Buddhism), highlighting the major tenets of the Yogachara school in ten chapters. It is considered his masterpiece and survives in one Tibetan and four Chinese translations. His second most important book *Abhidharma-samuccaya* presents a short summary of the key Mahayana Abhidharma doctrines.

As per the Tibetan historian Tarantha: 'He (Asanga) spent twelve years in Sri Nalendra during the latter part of his life, when, in the winter, the *tirthikas* (non-Buddhist heretics) came every day to challenge him in debate. He refuted their views and thus humbled them. Then he preached the doctrine to them. He conferred ordination on about a thousand [converted] *tirthikas*. He reformed, according to the doctrine, all the monks of all the monasteries who had fallen from the right view, right conduct (slid), right practices (carya) and right observances (viilhi) and made them extremely pure. At last he passed away in the city of Rajagriha, where his disciples built a chaitya with his relics'.[2]

Vasubandhu (c. fourth–fifth century. CE) was from Gandhara and is best known for founding the Yogachara school of philosophy along with his half-brother Asanga. As per Tibetan historian Taranatha: 'He (Vasubandhu) was ordained in Sri Nalendra and thoroughly studied the three Sravaka-pitakas. Moreover, he went to Kashmir and studied mainly under acharya Samghabhadra for a deep understanding of the Abhidharma and for learning the views of the eighteen schools and all the branches of knowledge. After learning the Vibhasa, the scriptural works of the eighteen

schools—particularly where the Vinayas and Sutras of the
different schools differed, and all the works of the six systems of
tirthika philosophy and the technique of debate in its entirety, he
became a great scholar.[3]After the passing away of arya Asanga,
he became the *upadhyaya* of Sri Nalendra'.[4] 'However, as per
Buddhist historian Buston Rinchengrub, Vasubandhu received
his education in the school of Samghabhadra in Kashmir . . . after
that he came to Nalanda'.[5]

He wrote A*bhidharmakosakarika* (Commentary on the
Treasury of the Abhidharma), which is widely used in Tibetan
and East Asian Buddhism, as the major source for non-
Mahayana Abhidharma philosophy. With the composition of
A*bhidharmakosakarika*, Vashubandhu received the attention
and patronage of two Gupta emperors viz. Vikramaditya
(Purugupta or Skandagupta, 455–467 CE) and his heir Baladitya
(Narsimhagupta, 467–473 CE). The first scholarly contest of
Vashubandhu was with Vashurata, who was a grammarian and
the brother-in-law of Baladitya. Baladitya challenged him for
a debate in which Baladitya was defeated and converted to
Buddhism. Vasubandhu may have persuaded Baladitya to build a
monastery at Nalanda, which was named after Baladitya, and he
thus played a key role in strengthening and expanding Nalanda
Mahavihara.

Buddhapalita (c. 470–550 CE) was one of the great
commentators on Nagarjuna's Madhyamaka thought. He is the
earliest Indian Madhyamaka philosopher, specifically identified as
a proponent of the sub-school of Madhyamaka, known in Tibet as
Prasangika-Madhyamaka (The Middle Way Consequence School).
He received this designation in Tibet due to his use of a form of
reasoning that drew out the absurd logical consequences of the
philosophical rivals of the Madhyamakas when he commented on
Nagarjuna's root text on wisdom.

Aryabhata (c. 476–550 CE) was thought to have lived in Pataliputra and studied and taught at Nalanda. His contributions in the fields of mathematics and astronomy are immense. Considered the 'father of Indian mathematics', he was the most prominent mathematician at the Nalanda Mahavihara in the sixth century CE. The author of his seminal book *Aryabhatia*, he was the first mathematician to use zero as a digit, which simplified mathematical computations and gave birth to mathematical concepts, which later became known as algebra and calculus. His innovative work in extracting square and cubic roots, and applications of trigonometric functions to spherical geometry, is noteworthy. He was also the first to observe that the Earth revolves around its own axis and attribute the source of moonlight to reflected sunlight. His extensive calculations and observations enabled him to calculate the value of 'pi' to the fourth decimal point.'[6]

Dinnaga (c. 480–540 CE) was born near Kanchipuram and was one of the founding figures of Buddhist logic. He initiated the system of Buddhist logic and epistemology (*Pramana*). His thought had a great influence on the thinking of later Buddhist philosophers like Dharmakirti. His philosophy only accepted 'perception' (*pratyaksa*) and 'inference' (*anumana*) as instruments of knowledge. He also introduced the theory of 'exclusion' (*apoha*). His masterpiece is the *Pramana-samuccaya*. Dinnaga founded a tradition of Buddhist epistemology and reasoning, and this school is sometimes called the 'School of Dinnaga'. Dinnaga's tradition of logic and epistemology continued in Tibet, where it was expanded. The logical and epistemological insights of Dinnaga were adopted to defend the tenets of the Madhyamaka school. He also influenced non-Buddhist Sanskrit thinkers and set in motion an 'epistemic turn' in Indian philosophy. After him, most Indian philosophers were expected to defend their views by using a fully developed epistemological theory or in other words those who follow reasoning.

Dinnaga, for the first time, introduced 'Three-membered syllogism' (*Trairupya*) which was accepted by the Mimansakas and Navya Naiyayikas, the followers of other ancient schools of Indian philosophy. Later, Dinanga further reduced Three-membered syllogism to Two-membered syllogism and ultimately to One-membered syllogism, which was supported by Nalanda masters such as Dharmakirti and Santiraksita.[7]

Bhavaviveka (c. 500–578 CE) was a monk at Nalanda who criticized Madhyamaka master Buddhapalita and argued that a proper Madhyamaka scholar should establish the view of Shunyata with *svatantranumana*, autonomous inferences, rather than just exposing the absurdities of one's opponent's views. He is considered in Tibet as the 'founder' and primary proponent of a sub-school of Madhyamaka known as *Svatantrika-Madhyamaka,* the Middle Way Autonomy school.

Chandrakirti (c. 600–650 CE) was born in South India and had come to study at Nalanda Mahavihara where he rose to be its head. He wrote an extensive commentary on the works of Nagarjuna and Aryadeva. His two most influential works are the *Prasannapada* and the *Madhyamakavatara*. He offers the most precise vision of Nagarjuna's emptiness and Madhyamaka philosophy and is considered to be the main proponent of its 'Prasangika' sub-school. According to Geshe Kelsang Gyatso, the author of *Ocean of Nectar* Chandrakirti also wrote a commentary to Nagarjuna's fundamental wisdom titled *Clear Words* and a commentary to the *Root Tantra of Guhyasamaja* titled *Clear Lamp*. He engaged in scholarly debates with Chandragomin, a philosopher of the Yogachara school.

Sthiramati (c. sixth century CE) was a Buddhist scholar monk at Nalanda Mahavihara who founded the monastery of Vallabhi in Gujarat as per the records of Xuanzang, which is also confirmed by the Vallabhi grant of Dharasena I, probably a vassal of the imperial

Guptas. His contribution to the spread of Buddhism in Tibet is regarded as greater than that of his successors—Santirakshita and Padamsambhava.[8] It is believed that he was well versed in the Tibetan language and translated many works on Buddhism from Sanskrit into Tibetan. According to H.D. Sankalia, 'from a glance at the headings of the works written, translated, and corrected by Sthiramati, it appears that he was the first writer, after Asanga, the author of the Yogachara doctrine, to write on the Tantra.' *Sadanga Yoga* is his most important work. He is the author of the commentary on *The Thirty-Stanza Treatise on the Consciousness Only Doctrine*.

Gunamati (c. sixth century CE) was a Buddhist monk from South India who lived at Nalanda Mahavihara and played a role in founding Vallabhi Monastery in Gujarat along with Sthiramati, as per the records of Xuanzang.

Dharmapala (c. 530–561 CE) was born in Kanchipuram in the family of a high official and studied at Nalanda Mahavihara. He rose through the ranks to become the head of the great monastery and one of the greatest luminaries of Nalanda. As per H.D. Sankalia, 'He was a contemporary of the great Bhartrihari [9] and wrote the shlokas of the *Bedavritti* in collaboration with him. The sloka portion was composed by Bhartrihari, while the commentary portion is attributed to Dharmapala, teacher of the Sastra.'[10] Apart from his treatises on etymology, logic and the metaphysics of Buddhism, his four books are in Sanskrit, out of which only three survive in Chinese translation, which include a commentary on Aryadeva's four hundred verses. His role in keeping the flag of the Nalanda Mahavihara flying far outweigh his limited number of literary outputs during a time when Mahayana Buddhism faced repeated attacks from the Hinayanists, Samkhyas and Vaisesikas and other followers of less popular philosophies.

Shilabhadra (c. 529–645 CE) was the head of Nalanda Mahavihara when the Chinese pilgrim Xuanzang visited. He was the son of a king from the Samtata area of Bengal and arrived at Nalanda to study under Dharmapala and was ordained into Buddhism by him. He became a master of Yogachara philosophy.

In a letter to Shilabhadra, then head of the Nalanda Monastery, King Harsha wrote, 'Now I know that in your convent there are eminent and exceedingly gifted priests, of different schools of learning, who will undoubtedly be able to overthrow them (priests of the Little Vehicle). So now, in answer to their challenge, I beg you to send four men of ability, well acquainted with one and the other school, and also with the esoteric and exoteric doctrine, to the country of Orissa.' [11]

H.D. Sankalia writes,

'Shilabhadra surprised even the most sanguine of his supporters, when, at the young age of 30, he defeated, refuting by profound and subtle arguments, a heretic of South India, who had dared to raise his head against the renowned Dharmapala himself. As a reward for this most wonderful victory, the king (perhaps of Magadha) granted him the revenues of a village, in spite of the persistent refusal of Shilabhadra, who said, "A master who wears the garments of religion knows how to be contented with little and to keep himself pure. What would he do with a town?" But he had to bow to the will of the king, when the latter replied that the only way to encourage the scholars to press forward in the attainment of religion was the distinction thus shown between the learned and the ignorant in the shape of reward of revenues to the learned. But Shilabhadra, a true Bhiksu to his bone, instead of keeping the revenues for his own personal use, built a vast and magnificent monastery. This monastery of Shilabhadra, it appears, lay on the route from Patna to Gaya, for the pilgrims proceeded to Gaya (Brahma Gaya) from this monastery.'[12]

Shilabhadra composed the text *Buddhabhumivyakhyana*, which is now available only in its Tibetan translation.

Arya Vimuktisena (c. sixth century CE) was a master of *Prajnaparamita* at Nalanda Mahavihara. He authored *Abhisamayalankarakarikavarttika*, the earliest commentary on the *Abhisamayalamkara*, which relates it to the text of the *Perfection of Wisdom Sutra* in twenty-five thousand lines.

Dharmakirti (c. sixth–seventh century CE) is considered a major figure in advancing Buddhist philosophy through his most important and largest work *Pramaavarttika* (valid knowledge instruments), which is an elucidation of Dinnaga's *Pramana-samuccaya*. His other works are mainly a commentary on the works of Dinnaga. Dharmakirti was born in South India in Trimalaya (Tirumala) and had studied orthodox Indian philosophy, mainly Mimansa, which he refuted later in his works. He became interested in Buddhist philosophy, and came to Nalanda as a youth in search of a learned master. As per the Tibetan sources, he was ordained by Dharmapala and was taught by Ishvarasena, who was a disciple of Dinnaga. He became a teacher at Nalanda Mahavihara and devoted his life to writing a commentary on Dinnaga's works, teaching and participating in scholarly debates. He was also a very fine and sensitive poet. Poet and diplomat Octavio Paz, citing Dharmakirti in his book *In Light of India* says:

'The philosopher Dharmakirti reduces all rationalizations to absurdity; the poet Dharmakirti, facing the body of a woman, does the same to his own dialectic. Dharmakirti denied the authority of Buddhist scriptures (but not the words of the Buddha) and argued that we indeed perceive reality, but our perception is momentary and ineffable; with the rest of its perceptions the mind constructs phantasmagoric entities that we call past and future, you and I . . . In one of his poems, he uses the example of a young woman's body to prove the truth of Buddhist doctrine:

Proof

Her skin, saffron toasted in the sun,
Eyes darting like a gazelle.
——The God who made her, how could he
Have let her go? Was he blind?
—This wonder is not the result of blindness:
She is a woman, and a sinuous vine.
The Buddha's doctrine thus is proved:
Nothing in this world was created.'[13]

Prabhamitra or Prabhakarmitra (c. seventh century CE) was born in a royal family in central India. He attended lectures on *Saptadeshabhumi Shastra* by Acharya Shilabhadra and had a deep knowledge of both Hinayana and Mahayana Shastras. He was appointed as a teacher of Abhidharma at Nalanda. He visited China during the Tang dynasty at the request of the erstwhile Chinese emperor Taizong during 629–30 CE and carried translations of three important Buddhist texts assisted by nineteen monks, which are his greatest contributions to Chinese Buddhist literature.

Subhakarasimha (c. 637–735 CE) was born in Central India to Sakyamuni ancestors. At the age of eighty, he left Nalanda to visit the Chinese capital Chang'an during the reign of Xuanzong (r.713–756). He was a pioneer of Tantrism in China which was further strengthened by Vajrabodhi and his disciple Amoghavajra.

Vajrabodhi (c. 671–741 CE) was a prince of the Pallava dynasty. He was sent to study at Nalanda at a very young age. He mastered the art of making mandalas at Nalanda. He was believed to have acquired supernatural powers and was summoned to Kanchipuram to bring rain during a terrible three-year drought in 708 CE. He seems to have been sent to China in the year 711 as an envoy of the Pallava monarch Narsimhavarman III to the Tang emperor of China. He visited Sri Lanka, Sumatra (717) and Java (718) where he met his disciple Amoghavajra (705-774). A Vajrayana master, he translated eleven Tantric works during a span of a decade (723–732) and taught the secrets of Tantra to Amoghavajra and two other Chinese disciples. 'In the years that followed, Vajrabodhi and Amoghavajra joined the circle of Tantric Buddhist monks that had first gathered in Chang'an around the Empress Wu Zetian and which now enjoyed the patronage of her successor. In time they became some of the most prolific writers and translators in Buddhist history. They brought new Indic ideas of cosmology, reincarnation, drug prescription, astronomy, horoscopic astrology, ritual magic, calendrical computation and planetary predictions to the Chinese court from Nalanda, Pallava Kanchipuram and Sri Lanka.'[14]Vajrabodhi was also an adept artist, especially in the art of Pallava paintings. He passed away in China at the age of seventy-one.

Shantideva (c. 695–743 CE) was a Buddhist monk, poet and philosopher at Nalanda Mahavihara. A devoted follower of Nagarjuna's Madhyamaka philosophy, he is also known as Bhusuku Pa, one of the eighty-four mahasiddhas. Shantideva is believed to have been born in the Saurashtra region of Gujarat as the son of King Kalyanavarman. He was known by the name Santivarman. It is believed that he was not a very bright student and entered Nalanada Mahavihara in disguise. Legend has it that the learned monks of Nalanda often considered him a lazy and unworthy student. However, he proved them wrong by delivering his discourse on *Bodhicaryavatara* or *The Way of the Bodhisattva*, which is a long poem describing the process of enlightenment from the first thought to attaining buddhahood, and is still studied by Mahayana and Vajrayana Buddhists. His other important work *Siksasamuccaya* (an anthology for training) consists primarily of quotations of varying length from sutras given by the Buddha.

Shantarakshita (c. 725–788 CE) was the first luminary of Nalanda who was officially invited to visit Tibet by King Trisong Detsen, who founded Tibet's first Buddhist monastery, Samaye, with the guidance of Shantarakshita and the blessings of Guru Padmasambhava. His major works include *Tattvasangraha* and *Taitvasiddhi*. Shantarakshita strengthened a synthetic philosophy which combined Madhyamaka, Yogachara and the Pramana (logico-epistemological) philosophy of Dharmakirti into a novel *Madhyamakalamkara* (The Ornament of the Middle Way) and his own commentary on the text *Madhyamakalamkaravrtti* (The Auto Commentary on the Ornament of the Middle Way). This synthesis is considered the final major development in Indian Buddhist philosophy. In this short verse text, Shantarakshita critiques some key Hindu and Buddhist views and then details his presentation of the two truths doctrine. This presents Yogachara idealism as the superior way of analysing conventional truth while retaining the Madhyamaka philosophy of emptiness as the ultimate truth.

Haribhadra (c. 700–770 CE) was the last of Shantarakshita's disciples who wrote the most famous and commonly utilized of the twenty-one Indian commentaries on *Abhisamayalamkara* (The Ornament of Clear Realizations) by Maitreyanatha (c. 350 CE) and the Mahayana path system in general.

Amoghavajra (c. 704–774 CE) was from North India and had travelled to China along with Vajrabodhi. He was sent to India by the Chinese emperor for six years (741–746) to collect key works on Tantra in India, during which he collected five hundred Tantric texts. After his return to China, he was honoured with the title 'Repository of Wisdom' by the Tang emperor Xuanzong. The Chinese emperor conferred upon him many honours and granted him land to settle in China. During a span of twenty-six years (746–771 CE), he translated seventy-seven works in more than a hundred and twenty fascicles and succeeded his teacher Vajrabodhi as the second patriarch of the Shingon (Vajrayana) Buddhist sect in China.

Padmasambhava (c. eight-ninth century CE) followed Shantarakshita into Tibet and was the son of Indrabodhi, the King of Udayana, which is believed to be located in the Swat Valley. Leaving aside the folklore concerning his birth and early life, what is known of him is that he resided at the Nalanda Mahavihara when the Tibetan king sent an invitation to him. He was a prominent expounder of the Yogachara school. Perhaps Padmasambhava's greatest legacy was establishing the Nyingma sect—the oldest of the four major schools of Tibetan Buddhism. Padmasambhava founded Lamaism in Tibet and is now deified and celebrated there as the Buddha himself. 'From the work that Padmasambhava did in Tibet, namely, the spread of Tantrism, we can well imagine what a hold the Tantric faith must have had upon the intelligentsia of Nalanda in particular and of India in general or else how could a pandit of Nalanda, who was specially sent for, deliver no other message to the inhabitants of 'the roof of the world' but belief in magic and sorcery and worship of innumerable gods and goddesses and demons?'[15] He translated various Buddhist texts into Tibetan, along with his disciples and other translators.

Kamalashila (c. 740–795 CE) was a disciple of Shantarakshita and expanded the pioneering work done by him in Tibet by firmly establishing Lamaism and Tantric Buddhism there with some elements of the Bon religion. He taught Tantra at Nalanda and was a great philosopher and logician. His most important compositions are three texts titled *Bhavanakrama* or stages of meditation from which the Dalai Lama has taught several times. His other works include *Tattvasamgraha–panjika* (Commentary on the difficult points of the Compendium of reality), *Madhyamakalankarapanjika*, (Commentary on difficult points of the ornaments of the Middle Way) and *Madhyamakaloka* (Light of the Middle Way).

Chandrogomin (c. eighth century CE) was among the great luminaries of Nalanda, whose contribution to the development of Tantrism is of great value. His intellectual output is staggering as he wrote no less than sixty books in Sanskrit, including *Simhanada Sadhana, Mahdkdrunika Stotra, Raksha Cakra and Abhicdra Karman*. From the nature of his works on Tantra, it appears that he was active in the eighth century when Tantrism was at its peak in Nalanda. He wrote extensively on Tantra as well as on literature, grammar, logic, astronomy, music, fine arts and the science of medicine. He was so well-versed in logic that he attracted the attention of the literary world. His writings include *Letter to a Disciple* (*Sisyalekha*), *Twenty Verses on the Bodhisattva Precepts* (Bodhisattvasamvaravimsaka) and *Confessional Praise* (Desanastava).

Dharmadeva (c. 943–1001CE) was a monk at Nalanda Mahavihara who visited China in 973 and translated forty-six Sanskrit works during the period 973–981 with the name Fa-tien. Later, he received an honourific title and was renamed as Fa-hsian and translated another seventy-two works between 982–1001. Altogether, he translated a hundred and eighteen works. His own original works include poems and *dharani*s.

Atisha (c. 982–1054 CE) was born in East Bengal in a royal family as Chandragarbha and was given the name Atisha (peace) by the Tibetan king Jangchhub Ö. He was initiated into Buddhism by Bodhibhadra at Nalanda and deepened his knowledge by studying Buddhism under Dharmarakshita. Atisha travelled to Sumatra by sea and stayed there for twelve years to study Bodhichitta with the monk Guru Suvarnadvipa. After his return to India, he became the head of Nalanda Mahavihara and later of Vikramshila Mahavihara. His classic, *Bodhipathpradipa* (The Lamp for the Path to Enlightenment) is widely regarded as the root text on the graduated stages of the path to enlightenment found in Tibetan classics.

Buddhakirti (c. eleventh–twelfth century CE) was a contemporary of Abhyakara Gupta of the Vikramasila Mahavihara who flourished towards the end of the eleventh century and the beginning of the twelfth century.

Dhyanabhadra (c. 1289–1363 CE), also known as Sunyadisya, Chi-Gong and Zhikong Chanxian, was perhaps the last of the luminaries of Nalanda Mahavihara, who was ordained and studied under Mahayana scholar Vinaybhadra at the great monastery before its complete decline and abandonment in early 14th century.[16]

He travelled throughout Indian subcontinent and then went to Tibet, Yuan China and Korea, where it is believed that he founded a monastery on the patten of Nalanda Mahavihara. [17]

A poetic inscription on a stupa erected in the memory of Dhyanabhadra, by a certain Li Se, indicated that he died in Korea.[18]

He played a key role in spreading the tenets of Mahayana Buddhism in East Asia.

5

Foreign Scholars at Nalanda

Nalanda was truly an international melting pot during the time of its existence where scholars flocked from all directions. They either took the northern land route from China, Korea, Tibet, Nepal, Central and West Asia or the southern sea route via Java, Sumatra, the Straits of Malacca, the coast of Burma and Arakan, to Tamralipti (Purba Medinipur, West Bengal) on the eastern coast of India. Here, the voyage ended, and the scholars then proceeded on foot to Nalanda.

A large number of monks must have visited Nalanda over the centuries of its existence, though we only have the records of a few mentioned by Chinese monks Xuanzang and Yijing.

Chinese society was profoundly impacted with the introduction of Buddhism in China by the itenerant Buddhist monks, traders and artisans who carried Buddhist scriptures and relics of the Buddha with them. It set in motion a civilizational exchange between India and China that lasted centuries. Chinese scholars and pilgrims started visiting India to collect Buddhist texts and paraphernalia for the performance of rituals and ceremonies. They wrote detailed accounts of their spiritual journeys to India, providing valuable records of Indian society, various Indian rulers and accounts of the flourishing and declining monasteries at the time of their visit.

These travel records, when translated into Mandarin, contributed to the development of a benign image of India among a large cross-section of Chinese society, including the members of the Chinese clergy, as the sacred land of the Buddha inhabited by civilized and sophisticated people. It was in sharp contrast to the image of the rest of the world among the Chinese people as uncivilized and barbaric. It motivated Faxian, Xuanzang, Yijing and a horde of monks from China, Tibet, Central, South and East Asia to visit India.

Faxian(337–422 CE) was the first Chinese monk to travel to India. He was more than sixty years old when he embarked on his trip to India in 399 CE from the ancient Chinese capital Chang'an (present-day Xi'an in Shaanxi province), through the northern land route crossing the treacherous Taklamakan desert (in present-day Xinjiang Uyghur Autonomous Region of the People's Republic of China). During the fourteen years of his journey, he visited the major Buddhist pilgrimage sites in India, travelled to Sri Lanka and survived a precarious voyage along the sea route back to China.

In his book, *A Record of the Buddhist Kingdoms,* Faxian writes that the main purpose of his visit to India was procurement of Buddhist texts related to monastic rules (*i.e., Vinaya,*) which was very much needed in China at that time. In the centuries preceding the journey of Faxian to India, a number of important Buddhist texts had been translated into Chinese. Kumarjiva settled in Chang'an in 401 CE and headed a team of translators to translate Buddhist texts from Sanskrit into Chinese just two years after Faxian started his journey to India. Kumarjiva introduced Nagarjuna's Madhyamaka school of Buddhist philosophy to China, which came to be known as Sanlun or Three Treatise

School. Although Buddhism was introduced in China in the second century CE during the Han dynasty, Kumarjiva's readable and smooth translation had revolutionized Chinese Buddhism. However, the growing Buddhist community in China needed original texts essential for the establishment and proper functioning of monastic institutions.

As Faxian journeyed west, he came across people who dressed like the Chinese but followed the customs of India in the city of Loulan in the Tarim Basin, which was already a major centre of Buddhism. He found the local Buddhist clergy reading Indian Buddhist scriptures and speaking Indian languages. Khotan, another major centre for Buddhism on the famous Silk Route on the southern rim of the Taklamakan desert is described by Faxian, 'Throughout the country the houses of the people stand apart like (separate) stars, and each family has a small tope (i.e., pagoda) in front of its door. The smallest of these may be twenty cubits high, or rather more. They make (in monasteries) rooms for monks from all quarters, the use of which is given to traveling monks who may arrive and are provided with whatever else they require.'[1] Faxian was given lodging at the Gomati Vihara in Khotan, which had 3000 monks residing there.

Faxian highlights life at Buddhist monasteries, the legends associated with them, the approximate number of monks living there, the rituals performed by them, veneration of the Buddha's relics in these places and so on in his book.

He began his journey from Chang'an, passed through Lanzhou, Dunhuang, Loulan, Karashahr, Khotan, Tashkurgan, Darel, Udyana, Taxila, Jalalabad, Peshawar, Bannu, Mathura, Sankisa, Shravasti, Kapilvastu, Sarnath, Bodhgaya, Rajagriha, Nala (Nalanda), Pataliputra, Vaishali, Tamralipti, Sri Lanka, Palembang (Indonesia), Quingzhou, Yangzhou and Nanzing.

It is interesting to note that Faxian travelled to India via the northern land route, but returned to China via the southern sea route sometime in 408 or 409 CE. on a merchant ship from the port of Tamralipti, in eastern India, to Sri Lanka, where he stayed for two years before boarding a seagoing vessel to return to China through Indonesia.

Faxian had turned seventy-seven when he reached Quinzhou. His book *A Record of the Buddhist Kingdoms* became a first-hand account of Buddhist practices along the Silk Route in Xinjiang, Afghanistan, India and Sri Lanka. Written in Mandarin, it became an instant hit among the elite of China including the Buddhist clergy who considered India as a holy land.

Faxian visited India in the company of scholars, whom he names as Hwuy-king, Tao-ching, Hwuy-tah and Hwuy-wei. While on his travels in India, he met 'a Tartar who was an earnest follower of the Law', and went out on the same mission as his, and then another band of five pilgrims in pursuit of the same religious purpose. Daozheng (Tao-ching), one of the traveling companions of Faxian, decided to stay in India and never to return to China, even in the subsequent births, and uttered these words, 'From this time forth till I come to the state of the Buddha, let me not be born in the frontier land'.[2]

Faxian does not mention Nalanda in his book directly, but he says, 'A Yojana south-west from this place (Rajagriha) brought them to the village of Nala, where Shariputra was born, and to which also he returned and attained his Parinirvana. Over the spot (where his body was burned) there was built a tope, which is still in existence.'[3]

Although Faxian does not mention Nalanda, his description of the place exactly tallies with the description gathered from other sources and the question arises whether he speaks of Nalanda or some other place near it. H.D. Sankalia in his book *University of Nalanda* writes that Faxian may not have visited Nalanda at all—

'Now this Nala was one yojana, i.e. seven miles from Giryek (old Rajagriha) and the same distance from the new Rajagriha; and as Nalanda was also one yojana from Rajagriha one is tempted to identify Nala with Nalanda. But we learn from Faxian himself that Nala was the place where Shariputra was born and had died. And it appears that this Nala was no other than Nalaka, where according to Sudassana Jataka, Shariputra was born. It is thus clear that Fa-hien's Nala was not Nalanda as alleged, but Nalaka, an unimportant village, nala grama, as the Jataka expressly calls it. From this it follows that because Fa-hien (Faxian) did not visit Nalanda, he did not give us a good account of the place. And the reason why he does not give the correct name of Nalanda, was that he did not visit Nalanda at all. For had he really visited it, we are unable to understand why he should not give us the correct name of Nalanda when the place was known for centuries after the Buddha by that name. Why don't Hiuen Tsiang (Xuanzang) and I-Tsing (Yijing) make any mistake in giving the correct name of the place? It cannot be said that Nalanda had become so insignificant that it had lost its original name when Faxian visited it and that it again recovered its original name when Sakraditya and his suit happened to see it and think of building monasteries there. On the contrary, the very fact that Sakraditya (Kumaragupta I) thought of erecting Sangharama speaks in favour of Nalanda . . . Nalanda was often visited by the Buddha and his disciples, and many discussions were held here with other religious sects. Here, the great Mahavira, the Jain tirthankara, met Gosala. So, long before the Christian era, the place was noted as a great religious centre. It continued to enjoy this fame even in the centuries after the advent of Christianity, because, as we have said previously, the place where all the philosophical discussions between Nagarjuna and others were carried on was Nalanda. Long before Sakraditya, Asoka had chosen this place for building a temple and a vihara.'[4]

He also adds that Faxian's records are often sketchy and brief and many of the records contain mere hearsay. Therefore, the silence of Faxian on Nalanda should be taken with a pinch of salt. The truth may be that he never visited Nalanda.

Xuanzang (602–664 CE) was ordained as a monk at the age of twenty, and seven years later, at the age of twenty-seven, he embarked on a journey to India in 629 CE.

When Xuanzang studied Buddhist texts in China, he found that they contained a lot of discrepancies owing to multiple interpretations of the Buddha's teachings. He realized that if there would be one complete version of the *Yogacharabhumi-sutra* (Discourse on the Stages of Yogic Practice), the disagreements arising out of multiple interpretations could be removed. A monk advised Xuanzang to go to Nalanda to study there. Xuanzang made the journey to learn the original teachings of Buddhism, collect Buddhist manuscripts to carry back to China and pay homage to the sacred places associated with the Buddha.

In 629 CE, the Tang Dynasty had plunged into chaos. King Taizong had usurped the throne by committing fratricide and forced his father to abdicate the throne. There was widespread civil unrest and subjects of the state were not allowed to leave the empire and travel abroad. Thus, when Xuanzang put in his request with the king for permission to go to India, the king refused to grant him the permission. Left with no choice, Xuanzang decided to go to India secretly. He got lost in the Mo-kia-Yen (Gobi) desert and wandered for several days. He almost lost hope of surviving when his horse miraculously led him to a spring and he was saved.

The route taken by Xuanzang passed through the Taklamakan desert, Turfan, Karasahr, Kucha, Tashkent and Samarkand, then beyond the Iron Gates into Bactria, across the Hindu Kush into Kapisha, Gandhara and Kashmir in northwest India. From there, he travelled to Mathura, Sarnath, Bodh Gaya and then to Nalanda, the holy land of Buddhism in the eastern reaches of the Ganges, where he arrived in 633 CE.

Xuanzang came across the central Asian kingdoms such as Yanqi (Agni), Kuchi (Kucha) and Khotan that used a modified Indic script. He recorded the Buddhist legends and miracles associated with the sites he visited and the Buddhist relics he saw on his way to India in great detail, as well as his interaction with the Indian ruler Harsavardhana.

Xuanzang's Reception at Nalanda

'On the tenth day he went to the Nalanda temple; the congregation there had selected four of their number, of distinguished position, to go and meet him; journeying in their company about seven yojanas he reached the farmhouse belonging to the temple. It was in (the village, where) this house (stands), that the honourable Maudgalyayana was born. Halting here for short refreshment, then, with two hundred priests and some thousand lay patrons, who surrounded him as he went, recounting his praises, and carrying standards, umbrellas, flowers and perfumes, he entered Nalanda. Having arrived there, he was joined by the whole body of the community, who exchanged friendly greetings with the Master, and then placing a special seat by the side of the *Sthavira* (presiding priest), they requested the Master to be seated. The others then also sat down. After this, the Karmadana was directed to sound the *Ghanta* (bell) and proclaim: "Whilst the Master of the Law dwells in the convent, all the commodities used by the priests and all the appliances of religion are for his convenience, in common with the rest.'"[5]

Servants had been instructed by the Mahavihara to look after every comfort of Xuanzang, making him feel at home in Nalanda.

After he had rested, he was granted an audience with Shilabhadra, the head of the University, during which he expressed the reason for his travel to India—to learn Yogachara and then he requested Shilabhadra to accept him as his disciple.

'Whereupon, following the rest, he entered to salute this eminent person. Having seen him, then Klabadra (the chief almoner) presented him with all things necessary without stint, paying his respects according to the proper ceremony, approaching him on his knees and kissing his feet, and bowing his head to the ground. The usual greetings and compliments being finished, Fatsong (Shilabhadra) ordered seats to be brought and spread out and desired the Master of the Law and the rest to be seated. When seated he asked the Master of the Law from what part he came; in reply he said: "I have come from the country of China, desiring to learn from your instruction the principles of the Yoga-Sastra."' [6]

'After the conversation, the Master took his leave. He was lodged on the fourth storey of the house of Buddhabhadra in the courtyard of the monastery built by King Baladitya. When the seven days entertainment was over, he was again lodged in the main chamber to the north of the house of Dharmapala with an increase in provisions. He was provided daily with Borneol incense and one *sheng*[7] of Mahasali rice. A grain of this rice was bigger than a black bean and when cooked it had a fragrance and delicious taste that no other kind of rice possessed of this quality. This kind of non-glutinous rice was produced only in Magadha and was not found elsewhere. As it was supplied only to kings and learned monks of virtue, it was called 'rice supplied to great persons'. He was also given a monthly supply of three sheng of oil and as regards butter and milk, he could take as much as he needed every day. Master Xuanzang had a servant and a Brahamana to serve him and was exempted from monastic duties; and when he went out, he had an elephant to carry him. Among the ten thousand native and foreign monks of Nalanda monastery, only ten persons, including Xuanzang, got such provisions. Wherever master Xuanzang travelled, he was always treated in such a courteous manner.'[8]

'The Master of the Law whilst he stopped in the convent, heard the explanation of the *Yoga-sastra*, three times: the *Nyaya-Anusara-sastra*, once; the *Hin-hiang lui-fa-ming*, once; the *Hetuvidya-sastra* and the *Shabdavidya* and the *Tsah Hang shastras*, twice; the *Prahvamula sastra-tika*, and the *Sata-sastra*, thrice. The *Koslia*, *Vibhasha*, and the *Shatpadabhidharma Shastras*, he had already heard explained in the different parts of Kashmir; but when he came to this convent he wished to study them again to satisfy some doubts he had: this done, he also devoted himself to the study of the Brahman books and the work called *Vyakarana* on Indian letters, whose origin is from the most remote date, and whose author is unknown.'[9]

Impressed by Xuanzang's zeal and devotion, Shilabhadra asked him to expound the Mahayana *Samparigraha-sastra* to the congregation and address the difficulties found in the *Vidya-matra-siddhi-sastra*. He attempted, in a work called *Hu'ui-Tsuiig*, to reconcile the two contradictory doctrines; that there is nothing to be attained by effort; and its opposite, that we may attain the one true nature by Yoga. The composition, when presented to Shilabhadra and to the assembly of eminent pandits, was very highly spoken of, and it was included in the curriculum for study.

He defeated the scholars of the Lokayata sect, who came to debate with the monks of Nalanda. In this debate, Xuanzang not only showed complete mastery over the various schools of thought in Buddhism but also a unique knowledge of the philosophical systems of others, viz., the Bhutas, Nirgranthas, Kapalikas, Jutikas, Samkhyas and Vaisesikas.

'Xuanzang carried 657 sacred texts comprising of 224 Mahayana Sutras, 192 Mahayana Shastras, 14 Sthaviravada Sutras, Shastras and Vinayas, 15 Maha-sanghika texts, 22 Mahisasaka works, 15 Samitya texts, 17 Kasyapiya works, 42 Dharmagupta works, 67 Sarvastavadin treatises, 36 Hetu-vidya treatises and 13 works on grammar. Out of his 75 works of translations, 40 translations were on Abhidharma treatises of various schools which are his most important contributions.'[10]

He is very meticulous in his descriptions of India's geography and climate, the measurement system, urban life and architecture, the caste system, the educational requirements for the Brahmins, the teaching of Buddhist doctrines, legal and economic practices, social and cultural norms and the eating habits of the natives. He also documents the natural and manufactured products of India.

Xuanzang's travel to India started a new phase in the spread of Buddhism in China and also for the first time established diplomatic relations between the Tang court and the various kingdoms in central and south Asia. His records also provide a valuable treasure of information on geography, art, history, archaeology and other disciplines of the places through which he travelled.

Yijing (635–713 CE) was thirty-six when he started his journey from China to India, in 671 via the southern sea route and arrived at the port of Tamralipti in 673. His main purpose to visit India was to improve the practice of monastic rules in Chinese Buddhist monasteries by copying the correct rules followed at the Indian monasteries, from 'cleansing after meals' to the 'regulations for ordination'. He understood the consequences of not practicing the original monastic rules such as 'the mode of eating', whether to use chopsticks or not, etc.

He stayed at Nalanda for ten years (675–685 CE) and recorded the customs and way of life of the monks and teachers of Nalanda Mahavihara down to the smallest detail. He collected over 400 Sanskrit texts, amounting to 5,00,000 slokas and translated over sixty texts into Mandarin including *Mulasarvastivada Vinaya*, Diamond Sutra, among other texts.

He divided eighteen Buddhist sects in India in the seventh century into four *Nikayas*. He had dispatched *The Record of Buddhism As Practised in India Sent Home from the Southern Seas* and the *Memoirs of Eminent Monks who Visited India and Neighboring Regions in Search of the Law during the Great Tang Dynasty* to China while he was still residing in the kingdom of Srivijaya (located in Sumatra, Indonesia). The first is a detailed account of how Buddhist doctrines and monastic rules were followed in India, while the second one provides sketches of fifty-six monks who travelled to India during the Tang dynasty (618–917). It was the first such compilation of the monks who had visited India over a century. It shows Yijing's talent as an anthologist in putting together a book of such high importance.

In his *Memoirs of Eminent Monks who Visited India and Neighboring Regions in Search on the Law during the Great Tang*

Dynasty, Yijing highlights that Chinese and Korean monks visited India in large numbers despite the perilous nature of the journey. Some returned to China while many died during their return journey or stayed behind in India.

His memoir provides short accounts of the lives of fifty-six Chinese and Korean monks who visited India in the seventh century underlining the devotion and desire of these monks to visit Buddhist sites and study at Nalanda.

Yijing was aware that many monks in China could not take the perilous journey to India and, therefore, in his introduction to his book *The Record of Buddhism As Practised in India*, he wrote: 'If you read this record of mine, you may, without moving one step, travel in all the five countries of India,'[11] and ended it with these words, 'My real hope and wish is to represent the Vulture Peak in the Small Rooms[12] of my friends, and to build a second Rajagriha City in the Divine Land of China.'[13]

This shows how much the Buddhist monks of China craved to visit India. Through the accounts of their journeys to India Faxian, Xuanzang and Yijing endeavoured to present the Chinese Buddhists community a vicarious experience of the sacred sites and events in the life of the Buddha. Moreover, they also brought with them the sacred Buddhist texts, relics and other paraphernalia, which helped in recreating an Indic Buddhist world in China—a second Nalanda, Rajagriha or Bodhgaya, where the Chinese followers of Buddhism could undertake pilgrimage in China itself without embarking on the long and perilous journey to India.

Besides Faxian, Xuanzang and Yijing, severals Buddhist monks visited India from China and Korea; some of them are mentioned by Yijing in his book *Memoirs of Eminent Monks who Visited India and Neighboring Regions in Search on the Law during the Great Tang Dynasty*. Many of them came to Nalanda.

Hyecho (704–787 CE) or Prajnavikrama was a Korean Buddhist monk from Silla, one of the three kingdoms of Korea, whose *Memoir Of The Pilgrimage To The Five Kingdoms Of India* in Chinese was found in the famous cave library in Dunhuang in Western China, and since then the text, the first and last part of which went missing, has widely attracted scholars' attention. His travelogue tells us that he studied at Nalanda Mahavihara, like so many of his East Asian fellow monks who went to India during the Tang period (618–917). He studied under Subhakarsimha (637–735) and Vajrabodhi (671–741). A Pala bronze discovered in Potala Palace, Lhasa has been discovered bearing an awkwardly inscribed Chinese inscription on an Indian piece of art that has some details about him.

Hyecho sailed to India in 723 CE and landed at Tamralipti and then proceeded for higher studies to Nalanda, where he stayed for three years. Here, he met another fellow Chinese monk, Shin-Kwong, a scholar from Ceylon who gave him a copy of the *Yogachara* and other sacred works. He left India via the northern land route in 729 CE.

Tao Hsi or Srideva belonged to the province of Shandong and came from an aristocratic family. He reached Mahabodhi Sangharama in Bodh Gaya after an arduous journey from China, spent a couple of years there and then proceeded to Nalanda and studied Mahayana. He was a great calligraphist and a man of literary talents. He made a gift to Nalanda Mahavihara of 400 Chinese Sutras and Shastras. Yijing could not meet him but was shown the chamber in which he stayed at Nalanda. He fell ill and died at the age of fifty at Amraka. After Tao Hsi's death, Yijing visited his room and composed a poem in his honour (words slightly rearranged):

This monk encountering much hardship
Reached India alone.
Honest at heart, he was
His only ambition—to propagate Dhamma
He could not lit the light (of Buddhism)
He never reached back home.
He died on the way.[14]

Shih-Pien or Sri Kasa was a native of Shandong, studied Sanskrit and Vidya Mantra, followed the path to north India and then from there, proceeded towards Amraka and received warm hospitality. He passed away while he was living with Tao Hsi.

A-nan yeh-po-mo or Anandavarman was a native of Hsin-luo (Korea). He began his journey from Kuang-hsieh, a small suburb, of the capital city of Chang'an. He studied Vinayas at Nalanda Mahavihara and copied many Sutras. He passed away at Nalanda at the age of seventy.

Hui-yieh or Jnanasampada was a Korean monk who stayed at the Bodhi Sangharama and paid great homage to the sacred relics of the Buddha. He spent some years in the Nalanda monastery where he studied Buddhism. While Yijing was reading and checking the Chinese manuscript of Liang-lun, he found that it was recorded by the Korean monk Jnanasampada—'Whilst dwelling under the Tooth-brush Tree, the Korean priest Hui-yieh wrote this record.' When Yijing enquired about him, the priests informed him that he died at Nalanda Mahavira the same year at the age of about sixty. The Sanskrit works he wrote were preserved at Nalanda.

Hsuan-t'ai or Sarvajnadeva was a Chinese monk who travelled to India via Tibet and Nepal during the Yung-hui period. He made a pilgrimage to the Bodhi tree and studied Buddhist sutras and shastras there. He visited many places in the Eastern region. He passed away at Bodh Gaya at the age of fifty.

Bodhidharma, a man of the Tukhara country (Bactria), of great bodily size and strength, first went to China and became a monk there. He studied Hinayana Buddhism. Afterwards, he came to India to adore the sacred vestiges of the Buddha. Yijing's account states that he met him at Nalanda. He was very fond of long journeys. From Nalanda, he again proceeded to North India at the age of fifty.

Tao-fang or Dharmadesa was a native of Ping-chou, China. He came to India via Nepal and stayed at the Mahabodhi Sangharama and even headed it for a couple of years before going back to Nepal.

Tao-Sheng or Chandradeva was a native of Ping-chou, who arrived in India in 649 CE via Tibet. He visited the Bodhi monastery and then went to Nalanda, where he was the youngest student. The King of Magadha honoured him on account of his young age. From there he proceeded east to Raja Vihara where he lived and studied Hinayana for several years. He carried with him many Buddhist texts, images and teachings of the Buddha. When he reached Nepal on his way back home, he got sick and died at the age of fifty.

Ta-ch'eng-teng Ch'an-shih or Mahayana-Pradipa came from Ai-chou, China. He became a monk at a young age. He followed T'an-su, the envoy from the Chinese Imperial Court and reached the capital where he was ordained to the Buddhist faith at Makaruna monastery. He reached Ceylon and then to Tamralipti and spent twelve years learning Sanskrit Sutras. He travelled to Nalanda and other Buddhist sites along with Yijing. He lived in the same old room where the monk Tao-hsi lived at Amraka. He passed away in the Parinirvana-vihara in Kusinagara.

Thonmi Sambhota (seventh century CE) was the son of Anu, a minister of the King Songsten Gampo of Tibet. He visited India for the purpose of studying Sanskrit and other Indian languages from Lipidatta, noted for proficiency in the art of writing. He learnt the sections of Nagari and Gatha characters from him and then proceeded to Nalanda Mahavihara and studied under the guidance of Acharya Devavidya Simha. While he was studying at Nalanda, the great Chinese pilgrim Xuanzang visited the monastery.

The texts that Thonmi Sambhota brought along with him are said to be the first Buddhist texts to enter Tibet from India. He devised scripts for the Tibetan language based on the Gupta Brahmi scripts which had been in use in India since mid-fourth century CE.

He simplified the Tibetan alphabet by shortening thirty-four consonants and sixteen vowels of the Gupta script into thirty consonants and four vowels in the Tibetan alphabet.

He also composed six texts on Tibetan grammar based on Sanskrit grammar.

Tang was a priest of the Mahayana School called Tang or 'the lamp'. He came to India by the sea route at Tamralipti, studied and perfected himself in Sanskrit and proceeded to Nalanda.

Tao-lin or Silaprabha was a native of Jiang-ling in Jing-zhou, Hubei, China. He decided to become a Buddhist monk at a young age and to travel to India to procure the original *Vinayapitakas*. He arrived in India via the southern sea route. He spent three years in Tamralipti studying Sanskrit and the *Vinaya*s of the Sarvastivada school. At Nalanda Mahavihara, he learnt Mahayana sutras and shastras and spent many years there mastering *Abhidharma Kosa*.

Hwui-Ta was a priest of Kung-chow. He arrived in India at Tamralipti via the sea route and then proceeded to Nalanda. He stayed at Nalanda for ten years.

Wu Kong travelled to India between 751 and 790 CE and studied Yoga, Kosa and other works, and died at Nalanda.

Wang Xuance undertook three or four journeys to India between 643 and 665 CE. His report has survived in fragments in the Buddhist encyclopedias.

Ling-yunor Chi-hing was from Ngai-chan in China. He engaged in painting Maitreya and Bodhidharma at Nalanda.

Wu-hsing or Prajnadeva was from Jiang-ling in Jing-zhou, Hubei, China. He studied the classics thoroughly and was considered as the most learned man in his province. He went to Nalanda with his constant companion Chih-hung and heard discourses on Yogachara and studied Kosa and the canonical rules of the Vinayas with great interest. Before his return to China, he completed translations of the Vinayas of the Sarvastivada school.

Once, Yijing and Wu-hsing climbed the Vulture Peak in Rajagriha and made devotional offerings there. They felt extremely grieved at heart when they looked towards their own land from the top of the mountain.

Yijing composed this poem expressing his feelings in mixed metres

We witness the transformation of the sacred
  mountain peak and glance at the ancient city of Rajagriha.
Thousands of years had already passed
but the water of the lake remains pure and clear
as it was before, and the bamboo grove
remains evergreen. The vague reminiscence
of the past had thrown back it's reflection

on the hard roads (of the city),
but everything is in ruins.[15]

Chih-hung or Mahaprajna The Vinayas master Chih-hung belonged to Lo-yang. He studied under the guidance of the Dhyana master Chi. He learned Mahayana at the Nalanda monastery. He studied the Vinaya Sutras composed by the monk Punyaprabha and translated them into Chinese.

Aryavarma was a Korean scholar from Silla who first came to Chang'an, China to study Buddhism. He studied in China during the reign of King Jinpyung (579–632) and went to India, leaving Chang'an in 638 CE and arrived in Nalanda where he studied the Vinaya and *Adhidharma* and copied many Sutras. He sought the teaching of the Buddha and stayed at Nalanda to pay reverence to the relics of the Buddha. But he passed away at the age of seventy at Musangsa in the Yongcheon area.

Hyeryun or Banyabalma was from Silla, Korea. After becoming a Buddhist priest in Silla, he went to study at Nalanda, showing deep reverence for the relics of the Buddha. He left Chang'an along with Hyunjo and the two arrived in India together. He had mastered Sanskrit and *Abhidharmakosaśāstra*.

Hyunjo went to North India with the help of the princess, Munseong of Bhota through Sarantaguk. He stayed at Nalanda for three years and learned *Madhyamaka Sastra* and *Satsastra* around 660 CE.

Hyeongak from Silla also went to China with Hyunjo and may have visited India with Hyeryun (Banyabalma). If they were together, he probably studied at Nalanda too. But it is said that he worshipped at Daegaksa in Magadha and died at the age of around thirty.

Hwi-Lun from Korea wrote a short account of the monastic establishments of Nalanda while Hiuen-Ta from Kung-chow spent ten years at Nalanda.

Wou-Hing or Wu-hing from Hainan, China lived till the end of his life at Nalanda and studied Yogacharabhumi and was instructed in *Abhidharma-Kosa*.

Other Chinese monks who visited Nalanda include Tche-hong, Ki-ye (970 CE), T'se-hoan, Huen-chiu and Hiuen-chao (around 650 CE). Ta-tseng-teng copied Sutras and Shastras and Hiuen-yen consulted Mahayana sutras.

Dharmasvamin (1197–1264) was probably the last foreign scholar to visit Nalanda before it faded into oblivion. He was a Tibetan monk who travelled to India between 1234 and 1236. His aim was to visit Bodh Gaya and to study the Buddhist texts with the Indian scholars. However, by the time he reached India, the Buddhist sites in eastern India had been destroyed.

According to Dharmasvamin's biography, when he visited Uddandapura (Biharsharif), it was the residence of a Turushka (Turkic) military commander. Vikramashila had been completely destroyed by the Turushka army. At Nalanda, there were eighty-four small viharas, which had been abandoned after being damaged by the Turushkas, and only two of the viharas were functional. Less than a hundred monks resided there, and a local king named Buddhasena of the Pithapati dynasty financially supported Nalanda's ninety-year head Rahula Shri Bhadra.

Rahula Shri Bhadra accepted Dharmasvamin as a student, and the two men translated Sanskrit Buddhist texts into Tibetan. Dharmasvamin mastered Sanskrit in Tibet under the guidance of his uncle and by studying the ninth century dictionary *Mahāvyutpatti*; his command over the language was so strong that he was mistaken for an Indian when he visited Bodh Gaya.

These are but a few monks who feature in historical records who visited Nalanda over centuries. The number of foreign scholars visiting the famed Mahavihara, about whom we may never get to know, must have been many times greater during its centuries of existence.

6

The Decline of Nalanda

The Gangetic plains of Magadha were undergoing political turmoil and a power vacuum after the decline of the Pala dynasty. This unstable situation was effectively exploited by the foreign invaders and their military commanders and mercenaries who started raiding the rich Buddhist monasteries of Eastern India.

Dr B. R. Ambedkar writes in his essay, *The Decline and Fall of Buddhism*—

'The disappearance of Buddhism from India has been a matter of great surprise to everybody who cares to think about the subject and is also a matter of regret. But it lives elsewhere. In India alone, it has ceased to exist. How could such a thing have happened? In dealing with this subject people fail to make a very important distinction. It is a distinction between the fall of Buddhism and the decline of Buddhism. It is necessary to make this distinction because the fall of Buddhism is one, the reasons for which are very different from those which brought about its downfall. For the fall is due to obvious causes while the reasons for its decline are not quite so obvious.

'There can be no doubt that the fall of Buddhism in India was due to the invasions of the Musalmans...Islam destroyed Buddhism not only in India but wherever it went.

Before Islam came into being, Buddhism was the religion of Bactria, Parthia, Afghanistan, Gandhar, and Chinese Turkestan, as it was of the whole of Asia. In all these countries Islam destroyed Buddhism. As Vincent Smith points out:

The furious massacre perpetrated in many places by Musalman invaders were more efficacious than Orthodox Hindu persecutions, and had a great deal to do with the disappearance of Buddhism in several provinces (of India).[1]

'Those who will pursue the matter will find that there were three special circumstances which made it possible for Brahmanism and impossible for Buddhism to survive the calamity of Muslim invasions. In the first place Brahmanism at the time of the Muslim invasions had the support of the State. Buddhism had no such support. What is, however, more important is the fact that this State support to Brahmanism lasted until Islam had become a quiet religion and the flames of its original fury as a mission against idolatry had died out. Secondly, the Buddhist priesthood perished by the sword of Islam and could not be resuscitated. On the other hand, it was not possible for Islam to annihilate the Brahmanic priesthood. In the third place, the Buddhist laity was persecuted by the Brahmanic rulers of India, and to escape this tyranny, the mass of the Buddhist population of India embraced Islam and renounced Buddhism. Of these circumstances there is not one which is not supported by history...

'Such was the slaughter of the Buddhist priesthood perpetrated by the Islamic invaders. The axe was struck at the very root. For by killing the Buddhist priesthood Islam killed Buddhism. This was the greatest disaster that befell the religion of the Buddha in India.

'There is therefore nothing to vitiate the conclusion that the fall of Buddhism was due to the Buddhist becoming converts to Islam as a way of escaping the tyranny of Brahmanism. The evidence, if it does not support the conclusion, at least makes it probable. If it has been a disaster, it is a disaster for which Brahmanism must thank itself.'[2]

The decline of Nalanda can be examined over a time span stretching centuries:

The immediate cause of the decline of Nalanda was the foreign invasion of north and central India and destruction of a network of Buddhist monasteries in Magadha (present-day Bihar) and the support systems that sustained these monasteries.

The intermediate cause of decline of Nalanda was resurgence of Brahmanical Hinduism which subsumed the Vajrayana or tantric form of Buddhism which had started resembling the ritualistic Shaivism. The deepening factionalism within Buddhism itself further weakened it by the end of the ninth century CE. 'The lack of cohesion and growing internal conflict within the Buddhists also contributed to their decline.'[3]

The long-term cause of Nalanda's decline was the protracted withdrawal of royal patronage to Buddhism. While Bakhtiyar Khalji's raids damaged the network and the support system of Buddhist monasteries in East India physically, the declining patronage and deepening political instability prevented the repair and establishment of new Buddhist monasteries.

'Qutub ud Din Aibak destroyed as many as twenty-seven temples before building the Qutub Minar. More violent still was the destruction meted out to the last Buddhist monasteries still surviving in Bihar.

'The fate of Nalanda is much disputed: it had been in decline for centuries and archaeology shows that it was burnt several times, with some of these conflagrations clearly dating to before the arrival of the Turks.'[4]

However, Anand Singh writes in his book *Nalanda: A Glorious Past*:

'The successive archaeological reports during the long span of excavations of the Nalanda monastic complex indicate vandalism, burning, and destruction of the complex by fire. Charcoaled walls, which were a result of fire, are still visible in the monasteries here. Charcoal, charred rice, burnt wooden logs, petrified bricks and walls are found peppered throughout the Nalanda monastic complex. Most of them belong to the Pala period. It shows that structures here were vandalized between the twelfth and the thirteenth centuries. In this regard we may cite some of the archaeological findings,

1. In monastery number 1, layers of ashes, potsherds, charred rice, along with a heap of brick debris belonging to the Devapala period attest to incidents of burning by fire and devastation.

2. Hirananda Sastri excavated monastery 1A and found burnt logs of wood and jambs showing the impact of fire on the door frames.

3. The shreds of evidence from chaitya number 3 suggest that it was destroyed by fire and occupants were so scared that in hurry they left behind their personal belongings.

4. In monastery number 4, burnt wooden doorjambs and petrified bricks show that it was destroyed by fire.

5. The burnt pieces of wooden stairs have been discovered from monastery number 5 and have been preserved at the Nalanda Museum.

6. Monastery number 6 has a heap of charcoal and burnt wooden columns in the uppermost strata showing evidence of camouflage by fire and burning.

7. A large quantity of heap of ashes and charcoal has been found in monastery number 8 showing that it was destroyed by fire.

8. The same shreds of evidence have been found in monastery number 9 where a large amount of ash deposits have been found from the wooden stairs.

9. There is evidence of destruction by fire in monastery number 10.

10. G.C. Chandra found a heap of charcoal, scattered pieces of charred wooden beams, and evidence of burning in every cell which attests to the fact that monastery number 11 was devastated by fire.'[5]

He further adds, 'The presence of a quiver and chainmail (chain armour of Central Asian design) at the monastic site suggests the presence of Turkish invaders.'[6]

Invasion of Buddhist Monasteries by Bakhtiyar Khalji

Bakhtiyar Khalji and his troops raided several Buddhist monasteries of Magadha. He even planned to loot the rich monasteries of Tibet to gather more wealth.

The evidence of burning and devastation of the Buddhist monastery of Telhara, which is in close proximity to Nalanda, has also been found during its excavation.

'The shreds of evidence of burnt wood, charcoaled grains, and ashes show that the monastery was burnt. Bakhtiyar Khalji used the stone and building material of the vihara to build the Sangi

Masjid. Subsequently, he moved to Odantapuri and destroyed it. After consolidating his position and establishing his administrative centre at Odantapuri, he and his soldiers prepared for an assault on Nalanda. It was not a spontaneous incursion but intentional and with full preparation.'[7]

The Persian historian Minhaj-i Siraj mentioned in his literary work titled *Tabaqat-i Nasiri* the invasion of Odantapuri by Bakhtiyar Khalji in 1197 CE. It was the two brothers Samsamuddin and Nizamuddin, who served Bakhtiyar Khalji and participated in the plunder of Odantapuri and Vikramasila, who recounted this to him at Lakhnauti, the capital of the Gauda Kingdom of Bengal. Minhaj-i writes about Khalji's attack of Odantapuri:

'He went to the gate of the fort of Behar (Odantapur) with only two hundred horses, and began the war by taking the enemy unawares. . . Muhammad Bakhtiyar with great vigour and audacity rushed in at the gates of the fort, and gained possession of the place. Great plunder fell into the hands of the victors. Most of the inhabitants of the place were Brahmans with shaven heads. They were put to death. Large numbers of books were found there, and when the Muhammadans saw them, they called for some person to explain their contents, but all the men had been killed. It was discovered that the whole fort and city was a place of study (madrasa).'[8]

Although there is no direct evidence of Bakhtiyar Khalji attacking Nalanda, his attack on the neighbouring Buddhist monastery of Odantapuri, which is in close proximity to Nalanda Mahavihara must have had an adverse impact on the supply and patronage on which it was dependent.'[9]

However, Anand Kumar Singh writes in his research paper
Decline and Destruction of Nalanda:

'Though Bakhtiyar's role in burning of Nālandā is
unquestionable, but not without doubts and suspicions that
it is but a prelude to the extinction of Nālandā Māhavihāra.
The much-hyped atrocities and debauchery of Bakhtiyar are
based on Minhaj-i Siraj's reference in *Tabakat-i-Nasiri* which
is widely quoted and misquoted amongst scholars. A closer
inquiry into the established hypothesis gets its overwhelming
support from Islamic sources but is not substantiated by the
archaeological and other contemporary records. In fact, both
the Muslim scholars of the medieval age and the Europeans
have exaggerated the incident to mould it in their favour.
After 1857, India's First War of Independence, the divisive
policy of British rule took root, and the history of India was
framed and argued in such a way that it has since become the
standard narrative. The Muslims who came from the West
were designated as foreigners and invaders who persecuted
the local inhabitants and destroyed their religious structures.
Under such circumstances, Bakhtiyar Khalji, a petty
plunderer, became for others a hero and champion of Islam.
Since the foundation of British rule, Western historians have
attempted to frame the history of the Indian sub-continent
to further their colonial interests which became more
profound and emphatic after 1857. The British government,
in analyzing the situation, held the Muslims of the country
responsible for the 1857 catastrophe.'[10]

Born in Garmser in 1150, Afghanistan, Bakhtiyar Khalji came
to India at a young age. He found some employment; however,
his services were soon terminated because of his disloyal and
unruly character. A few years later, he was employed by Maliq

Husamuddin Ughlubak, the commander of the Varanasi and Awadh regions, who assigned him the revenue of two villages for his sustenance, which enabled him to raise a band of mercenaries mostly drawn from the Khalji tribesmen from the eastern borders of Afghanistan.

When the Gahadavala dynasty (1089 CE–1197 CE) of Varanasi fell, central and north India, including Magadha and Bengal, fell into a political void and were frequently raided by foreign troops. The political vacuum in Magadha encouraged Bakhtiyar Khalji to raid the rich mahaviharas of Magadha, as he considered them to possess great wealth.

'The Tibetan Dhammasvāmī says Muslims have overrun Magadha, but yet were not successful in establishing a stable political system. The Muslim soldiers were roaming around Magadha causing consternation among the people by their loot and exactions. When Tibetan monk, Dhammasvāmī was returning to Tibet, he met two such soldiers in the ferry boat across the Ganga who demanded gold from him, and when he threatened to complain to the king, they became wild and snatched away the begging bowl of Dhammasvāmī. The matter was settled by Dhammasvāmī by offering some coins to the soldiers after the intervention of fellow Buddhist lay followers.'[11]

'Perhaps, the lust to plunder the monasteries of Tibet emboldened Bakhtiyar to make adventure into Tibet, though Minhaj says that Bakhtiyar recruited an army of 10,000 to invade Tibet and China which hints at the real purpose of expedition to monopolize the routes that carried a brisk trade in Tangan horses from Karambattan and Tibet to Kamrupa and from there to the district of North Bengal. But, the hazardous march coupled with the stiff resistance by the locals dampened the spirit of his troops, and he was compelled to retreat. The Kamarupa army drove him to the edge of the water and the whole army threw itself into the river desperately hoping to find it fordable, but its strong current proved fatal and carried away most of his troops. Though Bakhtiyar managed to reach the opposite bank at Devkot, he was stabbed to death by his own lieutenant Ali Mardan.'[12]

Bakhtiyar's greed for acquiring wealth through loot and plunder ended in his assassination by his own lieutenant. Nalanda was probably just one among the many monasteries he raided, which does not figure in Minhaj-i's chronicles. Nalanda survived his raids as recounted by the Tibetan monk Dharmasvamin who visited Magadha in 1234–36 CE and found Nalanda largely destroyed but still functioning. He stayed there for six months and gave an eyewitness account of the Mahavihara, stating that it had seven temples, fourteen large and eighty-four small vihāras which were damaged by frequent raids. Out of these, only two vihāras called *Dha-na-ba* and *Ghu-na-ba* were barely functional. The Mahavihara's perimeter wall was still intact, and the paintings of Tara and other Buddhist deities adorned its gates on the east and west side. Monks residing there had left for safer places. Only Rahul Sri Bhadra, the head of the Mahavihara, who was ninety years old, lived there with seventy Buddhist monks receiving education under him and a Brahmana disciple named Jayadeva. The Mahavihara received some patronage from a king of the Pithipati dynasty of Bodhgaya, named Buddhasena.

According to Taranatha, regular and sustained raids by the Turushka armed band massacred many monks at Nalanda and many fled in hordes. He adds:

'Paṇḍita Śakyaśri went to Ja-garsda-la (Jagaddala) in Odivisa in the east. He spent three years there, and then went to

Tibet. The great Ratanaraksita went to Nepal. Some of the great Paṇḍitas like the great teacher Ñanakaragupta along with hundred minor Paṇḍitas went to south-west of India. The great scholar Buddhaśnmitra and Dasabala's disciple Vajrasn, along with minor Paṇḍitas fled to the south. The sixteen mahantas including the scholars Saṅghamaśif Janana, Ravi Śri Bhadra, Candrakaragupta, along with two hundred minor Paṇḍitas went east to Pu-khan, Munan, Kamboja and other places. Thus, the law became almost extinct in Magadha.'[13]

Dharmasvamin writes, in 1235 CE, Nalanda was again attacked by the Turushkas of Odantpuri Jayadeva was arrested and put in prison by them, where he learned about their plan to raid Nalanda again. He succeeded in alerting Pandita Rahula Sri Bhadra about their plan, and all the seventy monks studying there left the Mahavihara except Dharmasvamin. He adds that both of them hid themselves in the temple of Jnananatha. A band of three hundred Turushka marauders raided Nalanda Mahavihara; however, they could not find them and returned with whatever they could gather.[14]

Built with burnt bricks, Nalanda Mahavihara, consisting of twenty-two large Viharas, eighty-four small ones, and seven temples, was gargantuan in size, and it was impossible to destroy it in one raid or even successive raids. Bricks are not suitable for the construction of mosques; therefore, they were left intact. Bakhtiyar Khalji was a raider and plunderer and had no interest in consolidating political power in Bihar and Bengal. Once the rich wealth of the Buddhist monasteries was looted, there was nothing more to plunder there.

As per the Tibetan accounts in the *Pag Sam Jon Zang*, 'a monk named Mudita Bhadra and later Kukuta Siddha, a minister of a

King of Magadha, tried repairing some of the viharas of Nalanda
Mahavihara, and Tārānātha mentions that King Cingalarāja
embraced Buddhism and made lavish offerings at the temple of
Nālendra, but did not build any viharas. Buddhism survived till
the 14th century in Bihar, Bengal, and Orissa.'[15]

'There is some evidence that Nalanda continued to function
in a much-reduced form until the early fourteenth century,
when the last Tibetan monks are described as coming to study
philosophy in its ruins. At that time, two small Viharas, out of
fourteen large monasteries and eighty-four small ones, remained in
serviceable conditions, perhaps rebuilt; seventy teachers remained
to pass on their knowledge to their students, having come to some
sort of arrangement with their new Turkish masters. Indeed, the
monastery apparently continued to receive modest support from a
few wealthy merchants, and from Buddhasena, Raja of Magadha,
who remained in place, having accepted the overlordship of the
Delhi Sultans. According to a Korean inscription the Bihari monk
Dhyanabhadra was ordained at Nalanda in the fourteenth century,
before taking up an appointment at the court of Mongol emperor
Kubalai Khan.'[16]

Resurgence of Puranic Brahmanism

Buddhism and Brahmanism have always been in rivalry since the
beginning of Buddhism. Among the kings of the same dynasty,
some adopted Buddhism while the others followed Jainism or
Brahmanism. Some kings followed Hinduism and Buddhism or
Jainism at the same time. For example, King Bimbisara is considered
to be a follower of Jainism by the Jains while Buddhists consider
him a devotee of the Buddha. Among the Mauryas, Chandragupta
Maurya adopted Jainism while King Ashoka adopted Buddhism
after the Kalinga war. The Gupta (third to fifth century CE) kings

were Hindus but were great patrons of Buddhism. Brahmanical Hinduism witnessed a great revival during the Gupta and post-Gupta (sixth to seventh century CE) period when Buddhism was also at its peak in central, north, and east India.

King Ashoka, who patronized Buddhism, was largely ignored in the literature of the Gupta age, and the Mauryans were depicted as Sudra kings.[17]

Mahayana and its evolution into Vajrayana at Nalanda Mahavihara brought Buddhism so close to Puranic Brahmanism that it became difficult to distinguish between them.

'The Purāṇas did commendable work for Hinduism to replace the ingredients of bhakti and personal god embedded in the Bodhisattva and the incarnation theory of Buddhism. The vamsa part of the Purāṇas was nothing but a rearrangement of the Buddhist ideology of Bodhisattvas and Sammāsambuddhas.'[18]

Sarvepalli Radhakrishnan writes in his book *Indian Philosophy*,

'The vital reason for the disappearance of Buddhism from India is the fact that it became ultimately indistinguishable from the other flourishing forms of Hinduism, Vaishṇavism, Śaivism and Tantrik belief. Mahāyānism was unable to acquire the prestige of primitive Buddhism, and so proved weak and vacillating in its conflicts with Brāhmanical religion...Throughout its conquests it did not aim at the suppression of other religions but tried to suffuse them with its own ethical spirit. Early Buddhism included Indra, Brahma and other divinities. The new converts carried into it much of their reverence for the old gods. The Hīnayāna accepted Brahma, Visṇu and Nārāyaṇa in their own names. The Mahāyāna, we have seen, never seriously opposed itself to the Hindu doctrines and practices. It elaborated the mythology and spoke of a hierarchy of divine grades and capacities, at the head of which was Ādi Buddha. While the Brāhmins

looked upon the Buddha as an incarnation of Viṣṇu, the
Buddhists returned the compliment by identifying Viṣṇu
with Bodhisattva Padmapāṇi, called Avalokiteśvara. Religion
became a private affair, and the Brāhmin ascetics were looked
upon as the brethren of the Buddhist śamanas. Brāhmanism
and the Mahāyāna faith affirmed identical philosophical
and religious views. The Mahāyāna metaphysics and
religion correspond to the Advaita metaphysics and theism.
In serving the needs of a large majority of men, it became
only a feeble copy of the Bhagavadgītā. A gradual process of
intellectual absorption and modification developed to such
an extent as to countenance the theory that Mahāyānism
was only a sectarian phase of the great Vaishnava movement.
The Hīnayāna, with its more ascetic character, came to be
regarded as a sect of Śaivism. Buddhism found that it had
nothing distinctive to teach. When the Brāhmanical faith
inculcated universal love and devotion to God proclaimed
the Buddha to be an avatar of Vishṇu, the death knell of
Buddhism in India was sounded. Buddhism died a natural
death in India.'[19]

Buddhist and Vaishnava deities started being worshiped together
at the same place in Nalanda and Bodhgaya, and the Buddha
started being treated as one of the incarnations of Vishnu. A
Vaishnav Buddha started being worshiped at the Mahabodhi
Temple. Buddhism was assimilated into Brahmanical Hinduism.
Numerous Buddhist places then turned into Vaishnava sites. The
hot water springs of Rajagriha, once a famous religious centre for
the Buddhists, became a place of Vishnu worship.

Buddhism and Brahamanism competed in the fields of
metaphysics and epistemology as well from the time of Nagarjuna
(150–200 CE), whose Madhyamaka philosophy claimed absolute
reality to be Shunya, therefore indescribable. The Naiyayikas and

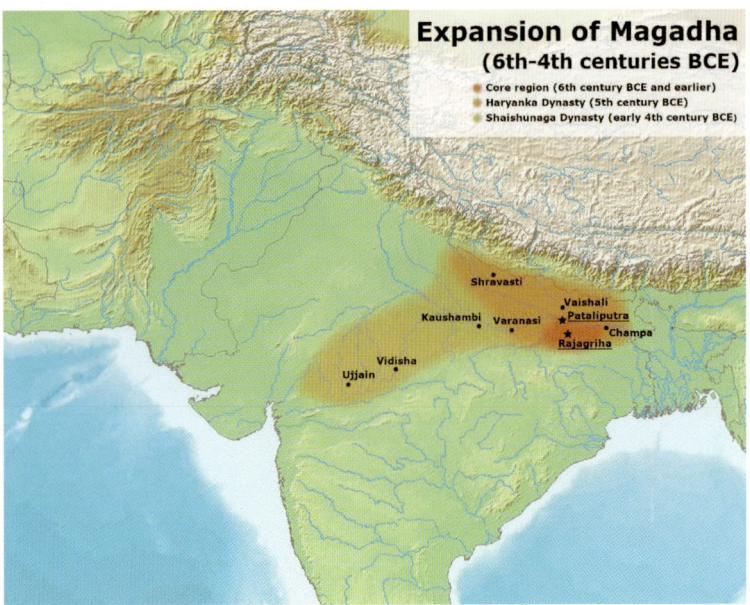

Map of the Magadha Empire

A panoramic view of Griddhakuta Parvat
(Vulture Peak), Rajgir

Sanskrit manuscript of the Heart Sūtra, written in the Siddhaṃ script. Bibliothèque nationale de France

A close-up of Vulture Peak, Rajgir

A view of Karandaka Pond at Venuvana, Rajgir

Ivory relief depicting Sariputra and Maudgalyāyana becoming disciples of Buddha

An image of Gautama Buddha with his chief disciples, Maudgalyāyana and Sariputra, with rice ears and straws, Bangkok, Thailand

Sanchi Stupa No. 3 where the relics of Sariputra and Maudgalyāyana were first discovered

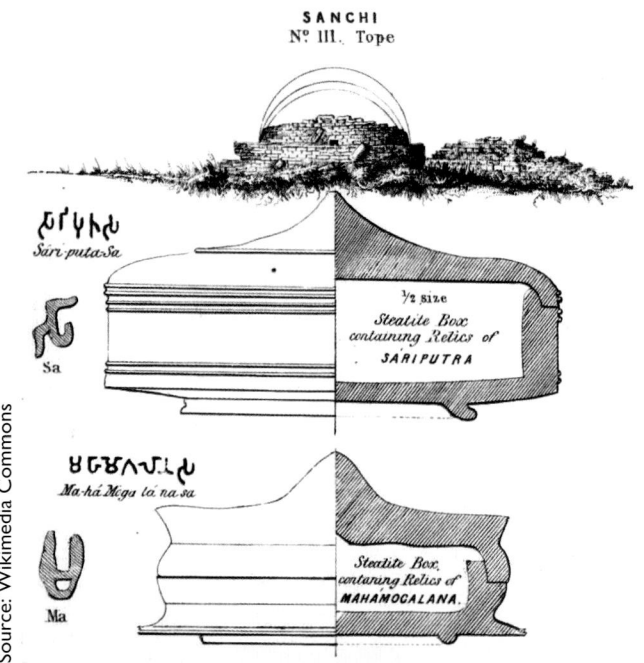

SANCHI
Nº III. Tope

Sári putaSa

Sa

½ size
*Steatite Box
containing Relics of*
SARIPUTRA

Ma-há Moga tá na sa

Ma

*Steatite Box
containing Relics of*
MAHAMOGALANA.

A sketch of the caskets containing holy relics of Sariputra
and Maudgalyāyana by Alexander Cunningham

Emperor Ashoka portrayed
on Kanaganahalli panel,
first–third century BCE

Kumargupta fighting a lion,
as depicted on his gold coin

Rear view of
the Baladitya
Temple in 1872

A statue of Gautama Buddha
at Nalanda found in 1885

An overview of Sariputra's Stupa site No. 3

An overview of the excavated remains of Nalanda

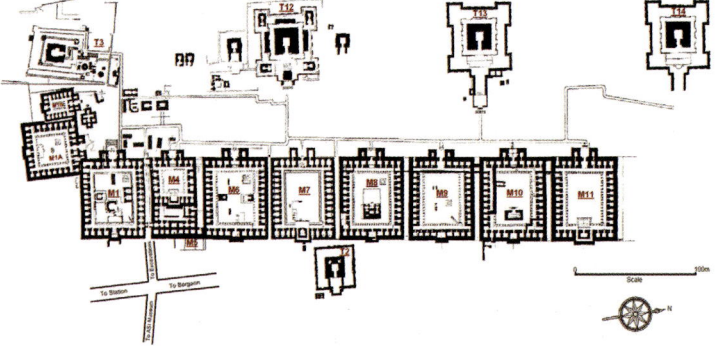

A sketch of the excavated remains of Nalanda

Detailed image of votive stupas

A replica of the seal of
Nalanda Mahavihara,
Bihar Museum, Patna

Copperplate
inscription of King
Devapala of Bengal

Votive stupas

An overview of a monastery

Temple No. 12

Details of pillars at Temple No. 12

The corner tower at
Sariputra Stupa at
Nalanda site No. 3

A stucco image
of Buddha

A stucco image of Buddha
in Dharmachakraparvartan
Mudra, Nalanda

An overview of Monastery No. 1A at Nalanda

Temple No. 14

Temple No. 13

An overview of Monastery No. 11 showing remnants of stone pillars

A spoke wheel
in the Stupa
Complex at
site No. 3

Burnt bricks at one
of the monasteries
of Nalanda

Nagarjuna

Xuanzang

Buddha in Bhumisparsha Mudra,
Bronze Alloy, Pala period, ninth
century CE, Bihar Museum, Patna

Prajnaparamita and scenes from the Buddha's
life c.1075, manuscript from Nalanda

Avalokiteshvara
Bodhisattva
from a
manuscript
from Nalanda

Avalokisteshvara in Khasarpana
Lokesvara form from Nalanda,
ninth century CE

Entrance of the Nalanda University established in 2010

Amphitheatre overlooking a pond at Nalanda University

Six-storey library at
Nalanda University

Auditorium, Nalanda University

Community Centre,
Nalanda University

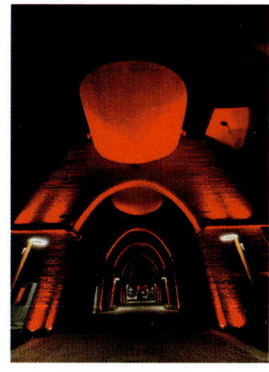

Nalanda University
at night

Exterior view of the Administrative Block at Nalanda University

Nalanda University at night

Interior view of Xuanzang Memorial

Xuanzang Memorial, Nalanda

Mimansakas were two major opponents of Buddhism during the time of Dharmakirti, who ruthlessly criticized both. Dharmakirti's scathing attack on Mimansa provoked his contemporary Kumarila Bhatta (seventh century CE) to write his *Sloka Vartika* to defend Mimansa and refute Buddhism, although he accepted the Buddhist Vijanavada (Yogachara) doctrine.

Shankara (eighth century CE) imbibed a great deal from Buddhist philosophy such as Madhyamaka and Yogachara, though he had reservations on some aspects of them.[20] Shankara was a spiritual successor of Gaudapada (sixth–seventh century CE), a Hindu philosopher and scholar whose ideas were a synthesis of Vedantism and Buddhism. In fact, his thinking carries some strands of Mahayana Buddhist philosophy; hence, he is also called *Pracchannabaudha*.[21]

Over forty important Buddhist thinkers from the eighth century CE to the first quarter of the thirteenth century CE, who lived in India, had a significant Nalanda connection; out of them, eight thinkers were active between 700 and 800 CE, seven between 800 and 900 CE, fifteen between 900 and 1000 CE and eleven between 1100 and 1200 CE, in India. During the same period, Brahamanism had only six thinkers who could match their repute.[22] These figures are based on a study conducted on data collected from the *Encyclopedia of Indian Philosophies* which clearly shows the intellectual edge Buddhism had over Brahmanism because of the influence of the Nalanda Mahavihara.

However, the bhakti saints started making a slow penetration among the masses in Bihar, Bengal and Assam, the areas which were strongholds of Buddhism, by borrowing its ideas and views. The kirtans of Chaitanya in Bengal and Sankardeva's in Assam won back the local people in the fold of Brahmanism.

'The *trikāya* doctrine of Mahāyâna and the *pañcavyūha* doctrine of Vaishnava were interpolated, and Vaishnava of Puri innovated *trivyüha* in the form of Krisna, Sańkarsana and Subhadra. Their art forms suggest that these were subordinate Vajrayâna deities who became Vaishnava deities. The chariot procession as mentioned by Xuanzang became a yātrā of Vaishnava deities, and finally the Lord Jnānanātha of Nālandā became Jagannātha of Puri.'[23] As per Monier Williams, a temple dedicated to Gautam Buddha, containing his relic, was dedicated to the Jagannātha form of Kanhaiya.[24]

> 'William Hunter, Alexander Cunningham, R.L. Mitra, H. K. Mahtab etc. have advocated that prior to its Vaishnavisation in the 9th century CE, the Puri shrine was a Buddhist shrine. Cunningham says that the Jagannātha triad represents the Buddhist triad of the Buddha, Dhamma and Sańgha as Dhamma is always represented as a female. The Term Jagannātha is often used in the treatises of two important siddhas of Vajrayāna order, viz. Indrabhūti and Anangavajra in their literature *Jainsiddhi* and *Prajñācaryāviniicayasiddhi* respectively. In both these works, Jagannātha has been invoked as the Buddha who is all pervading.'[25]

The Goraksa movement, a monastic movement founded by Yogi Gorakhnath in the eleventh–twelfth century CE, in Bihar, Bengal and Orissa was initially a part of Tantric Buddhism, which later seceded from it, and gave a Shaivite turn to the Natha cult (thirteenth–fifteenth century CE). The Tibetan text *Pag Sam Jon Zang*, written by Sum-pa Khan-po, helped in converting a large section of Buddhists to the Shaiva cult.[26] The Natha cult turned into Tantric Shaivism appropriating aspects of both Vajrayana and Shaivism. Luipa, or Matsyendranātha (ninth–tenth century CE) is considered as the founder of the Natha cult. He belonged to the Siddha sect of Yoginikula of Vajrayana and is still worshipped as Avalokitesvara in Nepal and as Shiva in India.

In Magadha and Orissa, the cult of Vaishnavism merged the boundaries of Buddhism and Vaishnavism.

Decline of Royal Patronage

Buddhism always needed some kind of patronage, as the monks were not engaged in any gainful economic activity or produced food, clothes and other basic necessities for themselves. Since the beginning of Buddhism, it had received the support of the rich merchants, as Xuanzang mentions in his accounts that 500 merchants purchased Nalanda for ten kotis (100 million) gold pieces and gifted it to the Buddha, who stayed at Pavarikambavana (the mango grove of Pavarika) for three months and delivered sermons.

Emperor Ashoka built a stupa and a vihara in Nalanda in honour of Shariputra who was born and achieved nirvana there during his reign in the third century BCE. The king or wealthy merchants often built sangharama and stupas for the community of monks. Sangharamas were managed by *aramika* (attendant) and the *aramika pesak* (superintendents).

Due to the emergence of Mahayana during the Kusana period (first–third century CE), the statues of the Buddha started to be donated at Mathura, Sravasti and Sarnath, which were also recorded at Nalanda but only during the Gupta period.

Nalanda received major patronage from the imperial Guptas. The copper plate inscription of Samudragupta (350–375 CE) issued in his fifth regnal year, mentions the donation of a village named Pushkaraka to Nalanda sangharama. Kumargupta I (415–455 CE) built a sangharama near the Great Stupa of Shariputra, and Skandagupta (455–467 CE), Purugupta (467–473 CE), and Narasimhagupta Baladitya (495–530 CE) also built viharas and temples in Nalanda.[27]

Harsha (606–647 CE), built monasteries and temples in Nalanda and granted village revenues to the Mahavihara.[28] Nalanda received revenues and daily necessities from over 200 villages bestowed upon the monastery.

The Ghosrawan stone inscription of Yasovarman(r. 725-752 CE) indicated that Yashovarmanapura vihara was built by the king Yasovarman of Kannauj and he made several grants to Nalanda Mahavihara.

The kings of the Pala dynasty, such as Gopala (750–770 CE), Dharmapala (770–810 CE) and Mahipala (988–1038 CE) were the last great patrons of Buddhism in India, whose donation inscriptions to Nalanda Mahavihara were found during excavations at the site. Gopala founded Odantpuri Mahavihara, while Dharmapala founded Vikramasila Mahavihara and Somapura Mahavihara.

The newly built Mahavihara of Odantapuri was only about ten kilometres from Nalanda, and it appears that it was developed as a parallel, if not a rival, seat of Buddhist learning along with the other Mahaviharas such as Vikramshila and Somapura, which must have taken away a number of eminent scholars from Nalanda.

After the end of the Pala dynasty, Brahmanical establishments started receiving the majority of donations, while some little grants were also made to the Buddhist monasteries. The Gahadavalas (1089–1197) of Varanasi were the last patrons of Buddhist establishments. The Gahadavala Queen Kumardevi of Kashi made donations to strengthen Nalanda Mahavihara.[29] The Gahadavala King Jaichandra (1170–1192 CE) studied under a Buddhist monk, but was a devotee of Krishna and the majority of the grants made by the kings of the Gahadavala dynasty were made to the Brahmanical establishments.

It shows a clear shift in the nature of donations from Buddhist institutions to Brahmanical institutions, which certainly impacted support to Buddhist mahaviharas such as Nalanda.

7

Nalanda's Contributions: How It Changed the World

While the edifices of Nalanda were largely reduced to mounds and the great monastery ceased to function in the early fourteenth century CE, its legacy in the development of science, mathematics, astronomy, philosophy, logic, religion, language, literature, art and architecture continues even today. The works, chronicles and records left by generations of scholars provide a rich testimony to these.

'Nalanda Mahavihara distinguishes itself as the only Mahavihara that has significantly contributed to all attributes of institution-building, artistic traditions, architecture, site- planning and developments in philosophy and systems of discourse and world religion (Buddhism) equally. The university-campus layout executed through combination of chaityas and viharas evident in its excavated remains is a turning point in development of pedagogical infrastructure of ancient and early medieval times. Witness to developments in systems of education, disciplines of Philosophy and Logic and doctrines (of Madhyamaka and Yogachara) that continues to influence Asia. No other educational establishment whose inception dates back to 3rd century BCE continues to guide scholasticism even after ceasing to function for eight centuries.'[1]

Evolution of the Vihara Architecture

'The genesis of Nalanda's institutional status began in the 3rd century BCE in the backdrop of Buddhist revivalism when Emperor Ashoka enshrined the corporal remains of Shariputra in a stupa (core of Site no.03 today). It is recorded that along with this stupa, the Emperor established a 'college' that, with the passage of time, became the Nalanda Mahavihara. Its physical infrastructure expanded with patronage from wealthy local *shresthis* (merchants) like Suvishnu. The contributions of the first generation of scholars in teaching the *abhidhamma* made the potential of Nalanda evident to patrons through whose support this Mahavihara assumed a gargantuan form. While scholars point to the lack of physical evidence of the viharas dateable to this phase, excavation at the site of the principal stupa or Site No. 03, has revealed a Mauryan stupa that, expanding through seven successive phases, culminated in the construction of a chaitya. It must also be mentioned that early viharas were constructed of perishable materials like wood, straw, mud etc. used only during *vassavassa* (rainy season) . These structures were built of permanent material only later when greater focus of the *Bhikshus`* life became education and in support of which patrons donated facilities, one of which was construction of viharas.'[2]

With the passage of time, the materials used for construction changed, and the quadrangular brick enclosure (as seen in Nalanda) became one of the typical designs of a vihara. Another variant in architectural style were the cave viharas.[3]

Both the rock-cut architecture found in cave viharas from the second century BCE and the square courtyard with the cell architecture of viharas, have roots in the Mauryan period (322-185 BCE).[4] The Barabar Caves in Bihar, the earliest known gift of immovable property for monastic purposes ever recorded in an Indian inscription is credited to Emperor Ashoka, and it was a donation to the Ajivikas.[5] By the second century BCE, a standard architectural for a vihara was established; these form the majority of Buddhist rock-cut 'caves'. It consisted of a roughly square rectangular hall, in rock-cut caves, or probably an open courtyard in structural examples, of which there were a number of small cells. The early stone viharas mimicked the timber construction that likely preceded them.[6] The Krishna or Kanha Cave (Cave 19) at Nasik has the central hall with connected cells, and it is generally dated to about the first century BCE. 'A clear idea of Vihara architectural plan can be obtained from examples in western India, where the *vihara*s were often excavated into the rock cliffs. This tradition of rock-cut structures spread along the trade routes of Central Asia.'[7]

> 'The development of the quadrangular vihara and the formation of the *panchayatan* chaitya remains Nalanda's foremost contribution to the sphere of architecture. The vihara which graduated from a single cell to a conglomeration of cells attained its quadrangular form for community-level residential-cum-educational facility in the Mahavihara of Takshashila by the 1st century BCE. At Nalanda, this quadrangular structure attained a regular form and was the hub of scholastic life...Each vihara had a centrally located courtyard which housed community level facility for conducting of daily classes, debates etc apart from being a stage for religious activities. Scholars have recorded that the

courtyard was pulsating with hundreds of pulpits placed for lectures to be conducted and debates to be convened. The raised platform on the eastern side of each vihara suggests that the same was a part of the educational facility where a distinguished acharya could assume his seat to conduct lectures or debates. The quadrangular form of the vihara crystallized in Nalanda was adopted and further elaborated in scale in the later Mahaviharas of Vikramshila (India), and Sompura (Bangladesh).'[8]

However, Christopher I. Beckwith claims in his book *Warriors of the Cloisters: The Central Asian Origins of Science in the Medieval World*, 'No pre-Kushan-period *vihāras* have been found, and the plan of the *vihāra* is strikingly different from that of the *saṅghārāma*, the typical earlier, strictly Indian, Buddhist monastic design. The *vihāra* design is thus a specifically Central Asian innovation developed under the Kushans and spread by them.'[9]

Commenting on Beckwith's claims, Johannes Bronkhorst, in his essay titled *Abhidharma across Buddhist Scholastic Traditions*, writes, 'These claims, and especially the second one, are not substantiated.'[10]

Beckwith's claim does not hold ground as evident from the aforementioned examples that the typical square rectangular hall architectural plan of the vihara had developed much earlier in India during the Mauryan times and travelled to Central Asia from there.

Beckwith acknowledges it: 'The earliest examples of *vihāras* built according to the plan of Adzhina Tepe (though without *iwāns*) have been found in the ruins of the great city of Taxila (Takṣaśīla), dating to the period of the Kushan Empire (ca. 50 Bc–Ad 225).'[11]

The square-rectangular courtyard structure of the Buddhist viharas, which is considered to have inspired the courtyard structure of colleges and universities across Europe, including the quads and courts of Oxford and Cambridge, developed during the Mauryan period and attained a regular form at Nalanda Mahavihara. The vihara plan was adopted and elaborated in scale across the world.

William Dalrymple writes in his book *The Golden Road: How Ancient India Tranformed The World:*

'The courtyard plan of these early Buddhist monastery universities was first described in detail by Xuanzang at Nalanda, and is still visible there and at early Buddhist sites such as the Kushan-era vihara of Adzhina Tepe in Tajikistan, the Gandharan monastery of Takht-i-Bahi near Peshawar and Taxila near Islamabad. From there it passed to Persia: in eleventh-century Nishapur, there were thirty-eight such madrasas pre-dating the founding of the greatest of these, the Nizamiyya, in 1038. Hence the idea of the college spread to al-Azhar in Cairo, then on across North Africa to al-Qarawiyyin University (now in Morocco), established in 956 and now recognised as the oldest living university in the world. From the Maghreb the idea of the college, and the courtyard plan of a vaulted cloister giving on to the rooms for the teachers passed north through Spain to Paris. Here, in 1180, was established the Collège des Dix-Huit, or the 'College of Eighteen Scholars'. Its founder was a wealthy English merchant, Jocius of London, who opened the college immediately after his return from Jerusalem, where madrasas built on the courtyard plan were once numerous. It was the oldest of the colleges which eventually became the University of Paris. The Collège des Dix-Huit, and its successor, the Sorbonne, founded by Robert de Sorbon around eighty years later, in or around 1257, retained the most essential characteristics of its direct ancestors, the madrasa, and before that the vihara, including the pious endowment that supported the student residents and professors, as well as a library and the courtyard form. So, from Paris it was only a short hop to the neatly clipped quads and courts of Oxford (which formally received its charter in 1248) and Cambridge (1264).'[12]

Evolution of College, Universitas and University

'Indeed, the idea of a university in the modern sense – a place of learning where students congregate near a well-stocked library to study a wide variety of subjects under several teachers – is generally recognized as having arrived in Europe via the Arab world...but where did the Arabs get the idea from?'[13]

In *Warriors of the Cloisters*, Christopher I. Beckwith writes that modern colleges have evolved from Central Asian madrasas, which are nothing but Islamized form of Buddhist monasteries, both having the same square or rectangular central hall architectural plan.

'It has actually been known for almost a century, though little recognized by most scholars, that the medieval Central Asian Islamic college, the *madrasa*, is an Islamicized form of the earlier Central Asian Buddhist college, the *vihāra*. The two are virtually identical in form, function, teaching program, and legal status. The identity of the unique architectural form of the Central Asian *vihāra* and *madrasa* has also been established by archaeologists. The typical Central Asian *vihāra* had a square or rectangular plan, which is replicated in the *madrasa*.'[14]

Dalrymple writes, 'Indeed the first ever recorded madrasa was built just a few days' journey from Naw Bahar (a Buddhist monastery near the ancient city of Balkh, Afghanistan) at Bost, in the unlikely location of Lashkar Gah, western Afghanistan.'[15]

According to Beckwith, the European Universitas, which were founded at Bologna (1088 CE), Paris (1150 CE) and Oxford (1167 CE) around the same time, were actually incorporated guilds of scholars, which could award degrees, and were completely different from the modern concept of a college or university.

> 'First of all, it is clear that the earliest three "universities"—the *universitas* guilds of Bologna, Paris, and Oxford—appear at approximately the same time in history, the late twelfth or early thirteenth century; regardless of scholarly tradition, none has been demonstrated with any certainty to be significantly earlier than the others. However, it cannot be overemphasized that although the Latin word *universitas* is usually "translated" as *university*, the early *universitas* was totally unlike a *university* in its purpose, structure, and functions. The word *universitas* originally meant an "incorporated" guild of any kind. Although the word *universitas* later acquired the meaning of a "guild of scholars" specifically, even then it still was strictly a guild; it was nothing like a university.'[16]

He further adds, 'The early *universitas* guilds of scholars did not own buildings or other physical property, they were not supported by permanent financial arrangements such as pious foundations, and they did not have much of anything else that we think marks an institution of higher education as such. The only significant thing the early *universitas* guilds did have that we would recognize as related to the function of a university was the right to bestow an advanced degree—the "license to teach"—and this has been shown to be a borrowing from the earlier attested *ijāza li-'l-tadrīs* "license to teach" of medieval Islamic culture.'[17]

Beckwith concludes that the modern University is actually the coming together of the vihara (college) and the universitas—

'But by the mid-thirteenth century, when the term *studium generale* came into general use, the *college* had already spread everywhere too. Its influence on the *universitas*, and vice versa, was such that a new institution developed out of both, namely, the University in the modern sense . . . The college was radically different in every way. Simple comparison of the medieval Islamic *madrasa* with the medieval European college has already shown that these two share their fundamental institutional features. Like the *madrasa*, the college is an all-inclusive academic institution with a permanent endowment recognized by the government. The endowment, in both the Islamic and Western European traditions, covered the expenses of the physical property and living support for the scholars—the students and their teacher or teachers—all of whom lived together in the same structure.'[18]

Going by the prerequisites required for a modern university as per Beckwith, Nalanda Mahavihara, fulfilled all the criteria of a modern university. The evolution of Nalanda from a vihara founded by Emperor Ashoka in the third century BCE into a Mahavihara with a well laid out plan with multiple monasteries, developed infrastructure, large endowments, its own walled residential campus, international students, where a variety of disciplines, including secular disciplines, were taught by the best scholars of their time, is how the idea of a university evolved in its true sense over centuries and spread to central Asia, Europe and the rest of the world.

Evolution of Recursive Argument and Scientific Method

Beckwith argues that the scientific method used during the first millenia of the common era was actually done through oral and written public debates, which used disputed questions or arguments followed by arguments method which he calls the recursive argument method, which is also known as the scholastic method.

Beckwith's contention in his book, *Warriors of the Cloisters,* is that this method of analysis and disputation developed first among Central Asian Buddhist scholars interested in disproving the beliefs of other Buddhist sects: 'The earliest text so far identified that uses a primitive version of the method, and indeed uses it throughout the text, is the Central Asian *Astagrantha* [or *Astakhandha*]. In this work, each topic argument is followed by a list of arguments about it.'

However, Johannes Bronkhorst in his essay *Abhidharma and Indian Thinking* asks, 'Does Beckwith not overemphasize the role of Central Asia? Is the *Astagrantha* (or *Astakandha*) really a Central Asian text?'[19]

Bronkhorst adds, 'Beckwith may not be right in thinking that recursive arguments do not appear in texts older than *Astagrantha* and the *Vibhasa*. The *Mahabhasya* of Patanjali is such a text, and it appears to use the recursive argument method. *Mahabhasya* is considered to be written in the second century BCE and is a commentary on the works of Panini and Katyayana. According to George Cardona, the *Mahabhasya* is composed 'in the form of dialogues in which take part a student (*sisya*) who questions the purpose [...] of rules and their formulations and an unaccomplished teacher (*acaryadesiya*) who suggests solutions which are not fully acceptable, and a teacher (*acharya*) who states what is the final acceptable view.'[20]

Hartmut Scharfe analyzes a passage from the *Mahabhasya* and concludes: 'With great stylistic art Patanjali has created the impression of a freely progressing debate with new disputants butting in now and then in which all possibilities of an interpretation are scrutinized. This is precisely what Beckwith finds in the *Astagrantha* and so many other texts. Since the *Mahabhasya* is older than the *Astagrantha*, it cannot have undergone direct influence of these texts.'[21]

Thus, it can be deduced from the evidence available that the recursive argument method, which led to the scientific revolution, was present in ancient Indian philosophical thought, such as in the works of Patanjali's *Mahabhasya*, and in Nagarjuna's *Madhyamaka*, which was a major school of philosophy taught at Nalanda Mahavihara. As Nalanda hosted such great scholars like Nagarjuna, Vasubandhu (the author of the *Vibhasa* whom Beckwith credits with developing recursive argument), Shantarakshita and Kamalashila (responsible for taking the recursive argument method to Tibet and other South Asian countries), it played a key role in advancing and further evolution of the recursive argument and scientific method over a millennia.

Mathematics and Astronomy

Based on Xuanzang's account, Nalanda Mahavihara had an observatory tower, which could have been used to track the movement of the celestial bodies and calculate time accurately.

Pataliputra (Patna), was the place of congregation of the mathematicians in India since the early fifth century. The famous Indian mathematician and astronomer Aryabhata (476-550 CE) was thought to have lived in Patliputra, modern Patna in Bihar and studied and taught at Nalanda. His work, *Aryabhatiya* produced the first systematic compilation of Indian mathematical and astronomical knowledge in a hundred and twenty one verses written in Sanskrit covering arithmetic, squares, cubes, square roots, cube roots, triangles, the properties of a circle, algebra, fractions, quadratic equations, spherical trigonometry and sines as well as the decimal system with place value.

'His extensive calculations and observations enabled him to calculate the value of pi–3.1416 –to the fourth decimal point.'[22]

'The ease of making calculations using this system had direct implications for astronomy and allowed Aryabhata to calculate the movements of the planet, eclipses, the size of the earth and, astonishingly, the exact length of the solar year to an accuracy of seven decimal points. Aryabhata correctly concluded, a full thousand years before Copernicus and Galileo, that the earth rotates about its axis daily, and that the apparent movement of the stars is a relative motion caused by the rotation of the earth, contrary to the prevailing view that it was the sky that rotated.'[23]

A hundred years later Brahmgupta, the author of the *Brahmasphuṭasiddhanta*, corrected and improved the work of Aryabhata, treating the zero symbol as a number just like the other nine, rather than merely as a void or an absence, and developed rules for using zero with other numbers. *Brahmasphuṭasiddhanta* was translated into Arabic in the eighth century and became widely known as *Sindhind*.

Nalanda's impact in the field of mathematics and astronomy was particularly significant in China as Amartya Sen notes: 'Several

Indian mathematicians and astronomers held high positions in China's scientific establishment.'[24]

William Dalrymple substantiates it in his book *The Golden Road*,

'Among the other Indians to rise to eminence at this time was the celebrated Gautama Siddhartha, the Supervisor of the Bureau of Astronomy between 665 and 698. It was his job to regulate the official calendar used in government and to interpret astral omens and other heavenly phenomena for the Empress Wu Zetian. As such, he was also expected to make the astronomical tables which could be used correctly to predict crucial celestial events such as solar and lunar eclipses, around which the religious and magical rituals of state were scheduled. Gautama was the first of three generations of his family who successively held the position; over that time his children and grandchildren married high-ranking officials. He was also the man in charge of making readings using the sophisticated planetary instruments brought together in the Mingtang (Hall of Light). For all these jobs he would have had to access the deep Sanskrit mathematical, astronomical and astrological learning for which the Indians were already celebrated not just in China but across the new Islamic world. Gautama put together a vast compendium of stellar omens entitled *The Prognostic Canon of Great Tang* based on the writings of the great Indian astronomical polymath, Varahamihira (505-87) of Ujjain; but he was best known for his Chinese translation of one the most important of all Indian astronomical treatises, the *Nine Planets*. This was valued for its accurate prediction of eclipses, and for containing several crucial Indic mathematical advances, then unknown in China, such as using a dot for zero and a

full table of sine functions. Nor were Gautama's family the
only dynasty of Indian astronomers employed by the Bureau
at this time: there are records of two other Brahmin families
of starwatchers at work in the capital at the same time, the
Kumaras and the Kashyapas.'[25]

Amartya Sen further elaborates, 'One of the connections on which
evidence of intellectual connections between China and India is
plentiful is the impact of Buddhists in general, and of adherents
of Tantric Buddhism in particular, on Chinese mathematics
and astronomy in the seventh and eighth centuries, in the Tang
period. Yiing, who was a student of Nalanda was one of the
many translators of Tantric texts from Sanskrit into Chinese.
Tantrism became a major force in China in the seventh and
eighth centuries and had followers among Chinese intellectuals
of the highest standing. Since many Tantric scholars had a deep
interest in mathematics (perhaps connected, at least initially, with
Tantric fascination with numbers), Tantric mathematicians had a
significant influence on Chinese mathematics as well.'[26]

Tantric Buddhist monk, Chinese Tantrist I-Hsing or Yi Xing
(672–717 CE), the greatest Chinese astronomer and mathematician
of his time, acquired great expertise in Indian writings on
mathematics and astronomy, dealt with a variety of analytical
and computational problems, particularly those concerned with
calendrical calculations and even constructed, on imperial order,
a new calendar for China[27] in which Indian astronomers located
in China were particularly involved and made a good use of the
progress of trigonometry.[28]

'This was also about the time when Indian trigonometry
was having a major impact on the Arab world (with widely used
Arabic translations of the works of Aryabhata, Varahamihira,

Brahmagupta and others), which would later influence European mathematics as well, through the Arabs'[29]

Beckwith writes in his book *Warriors of the Cloisters* that Yahyā ibn Khālid ibn Barmak (r. 786–803; d. 805), from the prominent Barmakid family who were hereditary Buddhist leaders (Pramukhs) of Kashmiri descent from Balkh, Afghanistan, the famous vizier of Harun al-Rashid, introduced Indian learning into the Arab world in the second half of the eighth century by bringing Sanskrit scientific books from India, along with Indian scholars to help translate them into Arabic. Under his direct, personal patronage, major works of Indian science were thus translated into Arabic in Baghdad. The works translated from Sanskrit included: The *Brahmasphuṭasiddhanta* (written c.628 CE) of Brahmagupta, which was the most advanced work of Indian astronomy available in the eighth century. It was translated into Arabic by al-Fazārī in 770 or 772, during the reign of the caliph al-Mansur (r.754–775), and became known as the *Sindhind*. It introduced Indian mathematics to the Arabs. Later philosopher and mathematician Muhammad ibn Musa Khwarizmi (780-850), who was from Persian-speaking Central Asia, translated the works of Aryabhata and Brahmagupta into clear Arabic prose. His most famous work titled *The Compendious Book of Calculating by Completion and Balancing, According to Hindu Calculation*, popularly known as *Kitab al-Jabr* became known as algebra. His sine table also derives from the trigonometrical chapter of the *Sindhind*. The *Sindhind* itself was reworked several times, most importantly by al-Khwarizmi, who based his *Zij al-Sindhind* on it but 'Ptolemaicized' the Indian system and made accessible the Indian innovations, such as linear and quadratic equations, geometrical solutions, tables of sines, tangents and co-tangents, to all.

Khawarizmi's name got associated with algorithm, an Indian idea that he introduced to the Arab world and subsequently to the west. The sources for Al-Khwarizmi's book on Indian numerals and mathematics using them, which is now known as the *Liber Algorithmi*, were translated into Arabic at this time, which included explanation of the use of the zero, rules for basic decimal system mathematics using Indian numerals and how to perform operations with fractions, including sexagesimal fractions, which were used in astronomical calculation.[30]

As William Dalrymple writes in his book *The Golden Road: How Ancient India Transformed the World*:

'From Baghdad, these ideas spread across the Islamic world. Five hundred years later, in 1205, Leonardo of Pisa, known by his nickname Fibonacci, returned from Algeria to Italy with his father. Fibonacci had grown up in a Pisan trading post in Bejaia, where he had learned fluent Arabic as well as Arab mathematics. Aged thirty-two, he wrote the *Liber Abaci*, the 'Book of Calculation'. It was he who first popularised in Europe the use of what were later thought of as 'Arabic numerals', so seeding the commercial revolution that financed the Renaissance and in time, as these ideas spread north, the economic rise of Europe. But these numbers were not Arabic in origin. As Fibonacci and his Arab masters recognised, they were Indian. "When my father held the post of notary at the customs house at Bejaia, he arranged for me to come to him when I was a boy,' wrote Fibonacci in the introduction to his *Liber Abaci*.

"Because he thought it useful for me, he wanted me to spend a few days there in the mathematical school, and to be taught there. Here I was introduced to a wonderful kind of teaching that used the nine figures of the Indias. With the sign o, which the Arabs call zephyr (al-sifr), any number whatsoever can be written. Getting to know this pleased me far beyond all else ... Therefore concentrating on this method, I made an effort to compose this book, so that those seeking knowledge of this can be instructed by such a perfect method and so that in future the Latin race may not be found lacking this knowledge."

The roots of these 'nine figures of the Indias' were first written down in the Brahmi script in third-century BCE Bihar, at the time of the Emperor Ashoka. This is something Europeans mostly erased from their memory in recent centuries. It is something they need to retrieve from oblivion today.'[31]

Philosophy

A number of schools of thought flourished in the Indian subcontinent from the 1st millennium BCE to the 1st millennium CE, which included six *astika* (orthodox) schools of thought in Hinduism, viz., Samkhya, Yoga, Nyaya, Vaisheshika, Mimamsa and Vedanta, which are known for their acceptance of the Vedas as an authentic source of knowledge.

During the same period, four non-Hindu schools of thought developed that rejected the Vedas as an authentic source of knowledge, which are known as *nāstika* (heterodox or non-orthodox) philosophies, viz., Buddhism, Jainism, Charvaka and Ājivika. While these schools developed through mutual criticism of each other, those following the Mimansa, Vedanta and Buddhism were the most popular, as they consistently engaged with society and attracted wider participation.

Four major schools of Buddhist thought developed by the third century CE. These were the *Vaibhasika* or *Bahyapratyakshavadi* (Realist) and *Sautantrika* or *Bahyanumeyavadi* (Representational or Critical Realist), both belonging to the Hinayana (lesser path), prevalent in Sri Lanka, Myanmar, Laos, Cambodia and Thailand, while the Sunyavada or Madhyamaka (Emptiness) and Vijnanavada or Yogachara (Consciousness only) belong to the Mahayana and are prevalent in countries practicing Mahayana Buddhism, such as China, Japan, Korea and Vietnam. Each school had a distinct definition of metaphysics (the branch of philosophy that examines the basic structure of reality) and epistemology (the study of the nature and grounds of knowledge).

At the Nalanda Mahavihara, the continuous engagement with *Yogachara* for centuries led to the evolution of a specialized school known as Mantrayana, Vajrayana or Tantrayana, based on the principles of *Yogachara* philosophy. It is prevalent in Tibet, Mongolia and parts of Russia.

A new philosophy synthesizing Madhyamaka and Yogachara and the logico-epistemology of Dharmakirti was developed at Nalanda Mahavihara by Shantarakshita, which is known as Yogachara-Madhyamaka.

Madhyamaka, Yogachara, Vajrayana and Yogachara-Madhyamaka spread across Central, East and South-East and South Asia and played a key role in shaping the practice of Buddhism there and the cultural and religious perspective of the people in these countries.

Madhyamaka

Madhyamaka means middle way. It is also known as Sunyavāda ('the emptiness doctrine') and Nihsvabhavavada ('the no essence doctrine'). Indian Buddhist monk and philosopher

Nagarjuna (c. 150–c. 250 CE) is the founder of this philosophy. His *Mulamadhyamakakarika* ('Root Verses on the Middle Way') is its core text of this philosophy. Madhyamaka philosophy influenced the evolution of the Mahayana Buddhist thought and practice throughout Asia. It entails that all phenomena are empty (*shunya*) of any inherent nature, substance, or essence (*svabhava*) and, therefore, cannot have independent existence because, as per the Buddha, they are dependently co-arisen. But this emptiness (*shunyata*) itself is also empty, which means that it does not have an independent existence, nor does it point towards a transcendental reality beyond phenomenal or observable reality.

Therefore, Madhyamaka shows that both absolute or eternal existence (such as the concept of Brahman or *sat-dravya* in Hinduism) and nihilism (the belief that nothing in the world has a real existence or meaning) are equally unreasonable and are the two extremes that it does not support.

The first extreme is *essentialism* or *eternalism* (*sastavadava*)—a belief that things inherently or substantially exist and therefore are worth desiring. Nagarjuna argues that we innately but naively perceive things as substantial, and it is this predisposition that is the root delusion that lies at the basis of all suffering.

The second extreme is nihilism or annihilationism (*ucchedavada*) encompassing views that nothing in the world really exists or has any meaning. *Madhyamaka* does not deny all reality like nihilism does, but only the apparent phenomenal reality surrounding us.

The goal of Madhyamaka is to end delusion and suffering, not by realization of emptiness but to help achieve understanding leading one to the path of liberation or nirvana. Madhyamaka occupies a central niche in all schools of Tibetan Buddhism and remains a potent force in everything from liturgical texts to philosophy to poetry.

Bodhidharma took Madhyamaka philosophy to China in the fifth century CE where he established the *Chan* or *Dhyani* Buddhism, which is based on Nagarjuna's Madhyamaka School.

'It influenced Kau Hwei-Wen who combined the key principles of *Madhyamaka* with the *Tai Chi Tu Lun* to establish the *Nan-ngo* and *Tsing Yuen* schools which form a unique philosophy of institutions. *Chan* remains one of the two living sects in China, the other being *Tien-Tai* through which Mahayana continues till date. The Sects of *San-lun-tsung*, *Pan-jo-tsung* and *Hsing-tsung* which bases its fundamental on *samvarti-satya* (conventional truth) of the *Madhyamaka* school influenced the socio-cultural life of the Chinese for more than eight centuries and have shaped the disciplines of history and philosophy in China apart from forming the crux of Tibetan Lamaism.'[32]

'In Japan, as many as eight sects (of the thirteen) namely Jodo, Jodo-shin, Yuzunenbutsu, Ji, Rinzi, Soto, Obaku and Nichiren were formed on the principles of the Madhyamaka school. Of these, the Jodo, Jodo-shin, Yuzunenbutsu and Ji comprise of the Pureland Buddhism Sect and has found great popularity among people of Japan. Of these Jodo became one of the most influential in the country. The Rinzi, Soto and Obaku are the three branches of Zen Buddhism (the word Zen is a transcription of the Sanskrit word Dhyana, meaning contemplation) and was introduced from China based on Madhyamaka principles. It found great followers among the Japanese warriors, enhancing their capability of controlling the mind. From the monochrome paintings (black and white), tea ceremony and ikebana to the formulation of Bushido (Japanese chivalry), Zen Buddhism has made significant contributions to the development of Japanese culture.'[33]

Yogachara

Yogachara is a Mahayana tradition of Buddhist philosophy that studies consciousness, cognition, and perception through meditation (*dhyana*) as well as philosophical reasoning (*hetuvidya*). Yogachara literally means 'practitioner of yoga.' Also known as *Chitta-matra* (mind only), *Vijnanavada* (the doctrine of consciousness), *Vijnaptivada* (the doctrine of ideas or percepts) or *Vijnaptimatrata-vada* (the doctrine of 'mere representation'), it formed one of the two most influential Buddhist schools of thought at the Nalanda Mahavihara along with *Madhyamaka*. It is primarily meant to help in the practice of yoga and meditation.

Asanga and Vasubandhu both (c. fourth–fifth century CE), from Gandhara along with Maitreya-natha are considered the founders of this school. 'The doctrines of Yogachara school crystallized at Nalanda travelled with its scholars to other lands, forming *Wei-shi-siang-kiau*, *Fa-siang-tsung* and *Avatamsaka* in China. These principles influenced the formation of Neo-Confucianism in *Shuyuans* (Academies of Classical Learning) of China and were subsequently practised in Japan and Korea. Yogachara formed the *Bkah-gdams-pa* and *Sa-skya-pa* schools in Tibet. The Bkah-gdams-pa school, followed by the 14th Dalai Lama himself, is the crux of Tibetan Buddhism, and its sub-sects, Karma-pa and Hbrug-pa, travelled eastward to Eastern Tibet, Nepal, Sikkim and further to Bhutan, respectively.'[34]

Vajrayana or Tantrayana

Vajrayana, also known as Mantrayana or Tantrayana, is a school of thought of Mahayana that evolved at the Nalanda Mahavihara and has its roots in the Yogachara philosophy practiced at Nalanda. It symbolizes the union of male and female, emphasizing the practice of indivisibility of wisdom and compassion. Its practice is characterized by *mantra dharani* (chanting), the making of mandalas (Buddhist devotional images) and *mudras* (ritual gestures), all of which were extensively used. While Tantrayana lost followers in India, especially in eastern India, after the fall of Nalanda and other Mahaviharas in Eastern India, it gained popularity in Tibet, Mongolia and East Asia. Acharya Padmasambhava (Guru Rinpoche) carried the Tantric Buddhist principles developed at Nalanda to Tibet. Assimilating the same with the local Bon religion, Acharya Padamsambhava made Buddhism acceptable to the wider society in Tibet, which accepted it as its state religion. He is also credited with having established the Nyingma school of Tibetan Buddhism, from which other schools of Tibetan Buddhism originate.

Yogachara-Madhyamaka

Shantarakshita (eighth century ce) combined Madhyamaka and Yogachara, the two major schools of Buddhist philosophy practised at Nalanda Mahavihara with the logic and epistemology of Dharmakirti and created a new school of Buddhist thought known as Yogachara-Madhyamaka or Yogachara-Svatantrika-Madhyamaka in Tibetan Buddhism.

Shantarakshita elaborated the new school of thought through the doctrine of the 'two truths': the ultimate (*paramartha*) and the conventional (*samvrti*), like other proponents of Madhyamaka philosophy under which all phenomena are seen as being 'empty' (*shunya*) of essence or inherent nature (*svabhava*) in the absolute or ultimate sense, while they can be said to have some kind of existence in the conventional, nominal or provisional sense.

Thus, Shantarakshita while describing ultimate truths follows Madhyamaka philosophy and while describing phenomenal truths, Yogachara philosophy.

The Skyflower Doctrine

The skyflower doctrine was developed at Nalanda Mahavihara. It simply means that all objective phenomena are only like skyflowers, unreal and vanishing. It is fully explained in the *Surangama Sutra*,[35] an influential Mahayana Sutra in Korean and Chinese Buddhism.

Logic

'Buddhist traditional logic and logical systems have found its first genuine expression in the works of Nalanda logicians, Nagarjuna and Asanga. Of these For its scientific development Acharya Dinnaga and Dharmakirti are credited.'[36]

Nalanda's luminaries played a key role in the development of Indian logic. For example, the Nyaya system of logic was the dominant mode of logic among Indian logicians, who considered Five Membered Syllogism (Panchavayaya Nyaya) as an ideal example of inference (Pararthanumana).[37] Different schools of Indian philosophy had different numbers of members of syllogism, viz., ten-membered syllogism and eight-membered syllogism, among others.

Contrary to the Panchavayava Nyaya of Gotama, Dinnaga, for the first time, introduced the 'Three-membered syllogism' (Trairupya), which was accepted by other ancient schools of Indian philosophy such as Mimansakas and Navya Naiyayikas. Later, Dinnaga further reduced the Three-membered syllogism to the Two-membered syllogism and ultimately to the One-membered syllogism, which was supported by Nalanda masters such as Dharmakirti and Santiraksita.[38]

Art

By the fifth century CE, Nalanda had become a major centre of art. Artworks produced at Nalanda had features of both Mathura and Sarnath with some local touch, which later evolved into its own distinct Nalanda School of Art during the Pala period by the eighth century CE and had a significant influence on the art of the east and southeast Asian countries

'Japanese pilgrim, the monk Ennin, noted that five of the esoteric images of the Buddha in the Jinge Monastery on Mount Wutai were modelled on images from Nalanda, possibly based on the statues brought from there by Wu Zetian.'[39]

The artworks produced at Nalanda can be divided into stucco, metal (bronze) and stone, depicting mainly Mahayana and Vajrayana deities.

Stucco Art

Stucco is mainly a mixture of lime, sand and mud, and occasionally gypsum, which is used mainly in the monasteries by the Buddhist monks for 'ornamentation, sculpting and as a finishing material, traces of which is evident at Site No. 01, 12 and 13 and in great detail at Site No. 03 at the excavated remains of Nalanda Mahavihara. Stucco art of Nalanda shows a high degree of finesse and syncretism between the iconography developed in the Sarnath School with themes of the Gandhara School. The finest example of such a fusion are the panels in the 5th layer of Site No. 3 depicting the Dipankara Jataka and Rahula's inheritance which show the assimilation of Gandhara themes with Sarnath features in stucco.'[40]

'Another characteristic development in the stucco art of Nalanda is the initiation of elaboration of the Buddhist pantheon. This can be noted in the increased number of Bodhisattvas accompanying the Buddha with their own retinues. With the gradual elaboration in rituals, these figures (Bodhisattvas and their retinue) received further definition gaining a distinct form during the Mature Pala period (10th -11th century CE).'[41]

As per Xuanzang, the colossal stucco images of the Buddha as high as eighty feet were installed in the sanctum of the chaityas at Nalanda Mahavihara, only remains of which are visible today. The eastern surface of the fifth layer of construction of the Great Stupa is adorned by scenes from the Buddha's life and Jatakas with Bodhisattvas and a figure of Tara are finest examples of stucco art in Nalanda. Nalanda stucco is known to have influenced Buddhist art practices in Thailand.

Stone Art

Nalanda was a major centre of Mahayana Buddhism, and as a result, the local manufacturing included stone sculptures of the Buddha accompanied by the Bodhisattvas and goddesses like Tara and Vajrasharda. The established Sarnath school blended with the local art traditions of Magadha, and sculptures that were done in stucco were now replicated in stone, such as the Buddha standing in *Abhay-mudra*.

This transition from Mahayana to Vajrayana is visible in the stone sculptures of Nalanda where new Buddhist deities appear with deep and refined carving. 'The figures on the other hand are comparatively less fleshy, slender, sometimes covered with a diaphanous drapery, tauter in appearance and stand in a *tribhanga* posture. This period also ushered in a new representation of the Buddha, depicted with a diadem or crown. This is considered an achievement of Nalanda artists'.[42]

Most stone sculptures of the later Pala period are inscribed and hence are paleographically dateable.[43] As per the Archaeological Survey of India report (1916–2001), a large number of miniature stone figurines used for veneration were found from the monks' cells of the Mahavihara. These images included statues of the Buddha, Bodhisattvas and panels depicting the Buddha's life.

Nalanda Bronzes

Metal art was prevalent in Magadha as the region is marked by inexhaustible sources of ore contributing to this art-form. The Pala dynasty facilitated easier and safer access to the copper deposits in Ghatshila in present day Jharkhand.

During the excavations of the ruins of Nalanda Mahavihara, over five hundred small bronze images dated eighth century or later, depicting the Buddha and Bodhisattvas, such as Avalokiteshwara and Manjushri, were found in the rooms of the monks, establishing Nalanda as a flourishing centre of metal works, especially bronze, during the Pala period (eighth–twelfth century CE). These bronze images have been kept at the Nalanda Museum, the Patna Museum, the National Museum and the Indian Museum Kolkata.

'Metallurgy (bronze) as an art-form was an integral part of the Mahavihara's curriculum. This is indicated by the presence of a brick-lined smelting furnace to the north of Site No. 13 and a large volume of metal figures recovered during excavation. These figures represent a range of deities of the Buddhist pantheon and show a distinct quality of casting technique and show careful syncretism of stucco and stone practices replicated in metal. Spanning between the 7th and 12th centuries CE, the metal art of Nalanda reached its zenith in the 12th century CE, and its pieces were carried to distant kingdoms of the Malayan archipelago, Tibet, and China by the scholars who studied at Nalanda. They carried back with them several pieces of metal figures, possibly because, compared to stone and stucco images, metal ones were less susceptible to disintegration.'[44]

Debjani Paul writes that although Nalanda bronzes lacked smoothness, they were often studded with semi-precious stones, which later became the norm of the bronze images produced in the Himalayan countries (Paul, 1987). The images had slender bodies, elongated limbs, a large head, slit eyes, and shallow cheeks, although the facial expressions and the robe draping had the influence of the Sarnath School. 'One of the earliest examples of Nalanda metal art is a figure of the Buddha in standing posture. Its elongated proportions, flat cheeks, large facial features, and bold expressions give the figure a boyish expression, showing all the classic features of Nalanda metal art dating to the 7th-8th centuries CE.'[45]

Tibetan historian Taranatha mentions in his book titled *History of Buddhism in India*, written in 1608, Dhiman and Bhitpala, father and son who were skilled artists during the reigns of Pala kings Dharmapala and Devapala. They are considered as the founders of bronze metallurgy in Nalanda.

Taranath writes in his book: 'In the time of King Dharmapala, there lived in Varendra an exceedingly skillful artist named Dhiman, whose son was Bhitpala; both of them produced many works in cast metal, as well as sculptures and paintings, which resembled the works of the Nagas. The father and son gave rise to distinct schools.'

Nalanda bronzes are said to have influenced the Javanese culture of Indonesia. AJ Bernet Kempers in his book *The Bronzes of Nalanda and Hindu-Javanese Art* examines their cultural influence over the art of Java. The Malay Inscription of Srivijaya, found at Talang Tuwo dated 684 CE, has some Mahayanist terms which belong to the Vajrayana tradition at Nalanda Mahavihara, as per the French historian George Coedes. The Chinese traveller Yijing visited Srivijaya in 671 CE for six months during his journey to Nalanda from China and back. In fact, the Buddhist kingdom of Srivijaya was used as a transit port by all the travellers from East Asia who visited Nalanda via the southern sea route. Its booming maritime trade with China and other South and South-East Asian countries must have facilitated easy maritime links with these countries.

Nalanda with its long-standing links with the Malay archipelago exercised a great influence on its cultural and religious life, including its art.

Miniature Painting

The Pala school of miniature painting flourished at Nalanda between the 8th to 12th centuries. It is one of the earliest examples of miniature painting in India, known for its illustrations of Buddhist texts, particularly on palm-leaf scrolls, and characterized by sinuous lines and subdued colors. The paintings primarily illustrated religious texts, particularly those related to Mahayana and Vajrayana Buddhism, including the *Astasahasrika Prajnaparamita* (Perfection of Wisdom in Eight Thousand Verses) and the Jataka tales. The paintings often resembled contemporary bronze and stone sculptures, reflecting a naturalistic approach, bearing some influence of the classical art of Ajanta. The miniature painting art developed at Nalanda spread to South and South East Asia where it continues to influence the local art traditions.

Architecture

'The development of the quadrangular vihara and the formation of the panchayatan chaitya remains Nalanda's foremost contribution to the sphere of architecture.'[46] Buddhist chaityas are primarily of two forms—the panchayatan (quincuncial form) and the cruciform. Of these, only rare examples of panchayatan chaityas have survived. 'Of these, the Mahabodhi temple and that of Nalanda are worthy and it is only the latter which retains the original brick and plastered construction from the 4th–11th century CE as opposed to the Mahabodhi temple which was largely reconstructed.'[47]

The principal shrine of a quincuncial chaitya rests in the centre of a raised quadrilateral while its subsidiary shrines stand on its four corners. The circumambulatory path peripheral to the principal shrine connecting the subsidiary shrines is called the *pradakshina patha*.

This quincuncial architecture is visible at Site No. 3 in the great stupa of Nalanda where a stupa was transformed into a chaitya through seven successive phases of construction over a period of seven centuries. 'Site No. 03 shows this transition of built form to attain the final quincuncial form, which was adopted for all construction and dates back to the 6th century CE.'[48]

'Some of the architectural designs developed in Nalanda have been copied in Borobudur. The stupas at Borobudur, Lauriya Nandangarh, and Kesariya have architectural similarity. It shows possible cultural linkages of Borobudur with these places which were facilitated by Nalanda Mahavihara.'[49]

The idea of making three-dimensional mandalas evolved at Nalanda with the Tantric Buddhist practices as part of the Vajrayana, characterized by mantra, dharani (chants), mandalas (Buddhist devotional images) and mudra (ritual gestures). 'The idea of building a stupa whose power was enhanced by surrounding it with a three-dimensional Mandala was an idea born in the vicinity of Nalanda, at the stupa of Kesariya in Bihar.'[50] Borobudur, the largest Buddhist temple in the world, is built as a single large stupa and appears as a giant Buddhist Tantric mandala when seen from above. 'There are quite a few design similarities between the Borobudur and Kesariya sites. Both sites have mandalas and life like Buddhas facing the sections of the universe. Both sites have hill-like mandala structures filled with Buddhist statues. This hints at the travel of ritualistic texts and ideas between the Pala and Srivijaya domains.'[51]

However, Anand Singh has a different view—

'The architectural designs of these stupas should not be confused with the Vajrayana or the mandala based structures.

Both Kesaria and Lauria Nandangarh are associated with the life events of the Buddha and the foundation of Nalanda was of the same age. The stupas with the terrace architecture were developed during the Gupta period.'[52]

Sanskrit

'From the literary resources of Nalanda it becomes clear that use of Prakrit and Pali was replaced by Sanskrit by the Buddhist teachers of Nalanda…the available Buddhist literature of Nalanda (in original as well as in translations) reveal that in Nalanda almost all literary writings were created either in standard Sanskrit or in the mixed or so called Buddhist hybrid Sanskrit. The philosophical texts, compositions on Buddhist logic, and ethical manuals composed by the Acharyas of Nalanda are in pure and Paninean Sanskrit, while *Stotras, Mahatmyas, Dharanis, Tantras* and *Sadhnas* were composed in hybrid Sanskrit. The works of leading teachers such as Dinnaga, Dharmakirti, Sthiramati, Dharmapala, Chandrakirti, Shantarakshita, Kamalasila, and Santideva bear testimony to the fact that Sanskrit occupied the most important position as the sole medium of all types of academic activities in Nalanda.'[53]

The Buddhist culture of ancient Nalanda, expressed mainly in the Sanskrit language, continues to be the most valuable world treasure and is undoubtedly the best contribution of Nalanda in promoting Sanskrit.

Translation

Today, most of the works of the great masters of Nalanda survive in either Tibetan or Chinese translations. Kumarajiva translated major works of Buddhism into Chinese. Following his footsteps, Xuanzang carried several Buddhist manuscripts to China and set up a translation bureau under his supervision in the seventh century CE. In fact, it was the writings of Xuanzang, which when translated into French, shed light on the existence of Nalanda Mahavihara. Without translations of the works of the scholars at Nalanda, it would not have been possible to preserve them, as the original Sanskrit and Pali manuscripts of many Buddhist sutras have been lost. The scholarly tradition of Nalanda has been preserved in Asian countries, such as Bhutan, Nepal, China, Japan, Mongolia, Siberia, Kalmykia and Tibet in translated works. Nalanda Mahavihara had a great repository of sacred Buddhist manuscripts at the great library Dharmaganja which was divided into three parts—Ratnasagara, Ratnadadhi and Ratnaranjaka. Scholars well versed in Sanskrit from around the world visited Nalanda, and they copied, translated and carried back home several literary works. The great tradition of the art of translation at Nalanda Mahavihara enriched the language, literature and culture of many Asian countries over centuries.

> 'The culture and language of Tibet is a living testimony to this tradition. From formulation of the Tibetan script (to receive knowledge from Nalanda) to the gradual establishment of Buddhism as a State religion replacing the Phon practices, Buddhism made an indelible mark on all facets of Tibetan life. Scores of manuscripts written by Acharyas like Padmasambhava, Acharya Shantarakshita, Asanga, Vasubandhu, Dharmakriti, Dinnaga, Gunaprabha, Sakhyaprabha, Buddhapalita, Bhavaviveka, Chandrakriti, Vimuktaseva, Shantideva, and Atisha, among others, remain some of the famous works that have not only enabled continuity of Buddhism but also preserved the knowledge of medieval India for posterity.'[54]

Poetry

Eighty-four Siddhas of Nalanda Mahavihara, along with the Jain saints, played a critical role in the development of Apabhramsa poetry from the eighth to the thirteenth century, contributing to new poetic forms such as *doha, chaupai, paddhari,* as well as *ulatabansis* or *ulatbani,* verses containing *virodhabhasa* (contrarian verses), which was also introduced by the Siddhas, and influenced the works of Kabir, Amir Khusro and Tulsidas, among others. They also started the tradition of using their name in the poem, which came to be termed '*Bhanita*' and has been carried on by the later poets and has survived till the present day.

As per Acharya Abhayakaradattasri, who compiled the hagiographic account of the eighty-four Siddhas in the Tibetan language, at least sixty-four out of the eighty-four Siddha poets hailed from Eastern India and as many as fifteen were specifically from Nalanda and Vikramasila.[55]

> 'Sarahapada was the first to compose mystic songs in Apabhramsa, a language that was the precursor of the modern languages of northern India. Nalanda played a key role in laying down the foundations of the Apabhramsa poetry. By the seventh century it had become a language of poetry although no actual specimens of such poetry have survived. Not only did a new kind of language take birth around this period, but so did many new metrical forms like *doha, chaupai, paddhari,* and so on. We find these for the first time in the works of Sarahapa and they continue to prevail till date particularly in Hindi.'[56]

The Siddhas thought that it was wise to spread their teachings in Apabhramsa, which was the language of the people in those days. Therefore, they chose Apabhramsa to compose their songs, although they continued to use Sanskrit alongside for intellectual discourse.

Apabhramsa, which means corrupt or non-grammatical language, originated in the confluence of Sanskrit, Pali and Prakrit. Hindi and other north Indian modern languages evolved from it. *Hindi Kavyadhara* by Rahul Sanskritayan published in 1945 has a selection of the surviving Apabhramsa poetry in which he has included the works of forty-seven Apabhramsa poets. Out of them, eighteen are Vajrayana Siddhas, from Sarahapa of the eighth century CE to Santipa of c. 1000 CE.

'Their adherents and the saint poets influenced by them continued to employ the vocabulary of the Siddha poets of Nalanda down to the fourteenth and fifteenth centuries. The most prominent example of such poets is that of Kabir. Not only does he use the Siddha vocabulary, but he often adopts the ideas of the Siddhas, sometimes verbatim. Take, for example, this doha of Kabir:

Jakà guru bhi andhalà cela khara nirandha /
andhai andha theliya dunyuñ Kupa padanta //

(Whose teacher is blind, the disciple is also blind /
one blind guided by another blind, the both fall into the well //)

This bears resemblance to the following Doha of Saraha which has the same meaning:

Java na apa janijai tava na sissa karei /
Andha andha Kadhava tima vennavi Kuva padei //

(One who does not know oneself, should not keep a disciple /
a blind leading a blind, the both fall into the well //)

Script and Grammar

Nalanda contributed to the development of the Tibetan script and grammar. Its alumnus Thonmi Sambhota devised scripts for the Tibetan language based on the Gupta scripts and simplified the Tibetan alphabet.

Book Culture and Dhamma Wheel

The evolution of Mahayana Buddhism democratized Buddhism, making it possible for a layman to aspire to become a Bodhisattva. Its foundational text, *Prajnaparamita Sutra*, which comprises over one lakh verses, was difficult for anyone to memorize and then transmit it orally to the next generation. It became necessary to write it all in a book format.

Nalanda played a central role in the development of the art of manuscript writing, illustration, preservation and copying. The manuscripts written on palm leaf scrolls were illustrated with the miniature paintings at Nalanda. The accounts of Xuanzang and Yijing provide vivid descriptions of the manuscript culture that thrived at Nalanda. Xuanzang himself carried 657 manuscripts from Nalanda back to China, while Yijing carried 400 manuscripts along with him.

The books were written on palm leaves, which were shaped into long, rectangular formats, where standard-sized folios were bound together with twines and surmounted by wooden panels.

They were written with a reed pen and black ink. The ink pots have been found during the excavation of Nalanda. The Nalanda Copperplate of Devapala refers to Nalanda as a sacred abode of *Prajnaparamita* and the writing of *Dharma Ratnas*.

Clothes, silk, baked bricks, and copper and gold plates were also used to write manuscripts at Nalanda.

The manuscripts copied at Nalanda were carried by the monks to distant lands and translated into local languages.

Thus, manuscript writing, copying and preservation culture at Nalanda accelerated the transition from an oral tradition to a written one. In fact, the first book ever to be printed in the world using woodblock printing in 868 CE is The Diamond Sutra *(Vajracchedika Prajnaparamita Sutra)*, which is part of *Prajnaparamita Sutra*.

It is believed that the *Prajnaparamita Sutra* was written by none other than Nagarjuna himself at Nalanda who, as per legends, is considered to retrieve it from the Nagas, centuries after it was delivered to Shariputra by Bodhisattva Avalokiteshvara in the presence of the Buddha at Gridhakuta Parvat in Rajagriha.

The Diamond Sutra was translated into Chinese from Sanskrit by Kumarajiva in 401 CE and it was his translation that was discovered in the Dunhuang Caves.

The book worship of Prajnaparamita evolved at Nalanda, which in due course led to the invention of Dhamma Wheels, in which sacred texts, or Dharanis, are mechanically revolved to produce religious merit.

'The Dhamma wheel was the genius invention of some socially concerned monks of Nalanda who thought of this easy device that could generate and share merits with all sections of the society, viz., nobles, clergy, and commoners. It began with the book cult of invoking the *Prajnaparamita Sutra* but later on, its scope was extended across all sects of Buddhism by inscribing the Tipitaka, the Patittyasamutapada, deities of Mahayana, and Vajrayana.'[57]

Medicine

'The history of the scientific genesis of the medical system indicates that the shift from the religio-magic to an empirico-rational system began under the leadership of the Buddhist monks. With the emergence of the Buddhist sangha, the modalities to take care of the health of the fraternity of the monks and nuns began to develop.'[58]

The Buddha underscored four basic necessities for the monks, i.e. food, clothes, shelter and medicine.

Nalanda Mahavihara played a vital role in advancing the practice of medicine for the welfare of the monks and the common people, foundation of which was laid down by Jivaka, the personal physician of King Bimbisara and the Buddha at Rajagriha.

In the Mahayana tradition, the Bhaisajya-raja and Bhaisajya-samudgata are the two Bodhisattvas of Healing and are the first major deities to appear in Buddhism.

Bhaisajya-guru Sutra was translated into Chinese by Xuanzang, Yijing and Dharmagupta.

Raksa literature and Dharanis were part of curing the patient's mind. Chikitsavidya was taught at Nalanda Mahavihara along with Shabdavidya, Shilpavidya, Hetuvidya, etc. as per Yijing, who gives a detailed account of medical practice followed at Nalanda mentioning Vagabhatta's *Astangahridaya* as the most important medical treatise to be taught there. It included eight kinds of teachings of medicine (*astanga*) in Nalanda, i.e. *salya* (cure of sores), *salakya* (acupuncture), *kayacititsa* (diseases of the body), *bhuta-vidya* (root out demonic forces), *kaumarbhrtya* (diseases of children), *agada* (a blend of medicine and surgery), *rasayana* (alchemy) and *vajikarana* (methods of revitalizing the legs and body).[59]

He says Hantika (yellow myrobalan), ginger, Yu-chin-bsiang (Kunkuma) and A-wei (asafoetida) were commonly used in India.

Myrobalan (Haritaki) was the most commonly used in Nalanda for treating ailments.

It was an astringent, thermogenic, soothing, anti-inflammatory, vulnerary (curing eruptions), gastric, purgative, digestive, parasiticidal, cardiotonic, aphrodisiac, antiseptic, diuretic, febrifuge, depurative, and general therapeutic.

It was used to heal wounds, ulcers, inflammations, gastric disorders, anorexia, helminthiasis, flatulence, hemorrhoids, jaundice, hepatopathy, hiccups, coughs, uropathy, vesical, and renal calculi. It was also helpful in headaches, epilepsy, ophthalmopathy, skin diseases, high fever, cardiac issues, stomatitis, neuropathy, and general weakness.

The chebulic myrobalan is extensively used in combination with the belleric (lerminalia bellirica) and embolic myrobalan (Phyllanthu semblica) as triphala (three fruits-popularly known as avanla, harr, and baheda). It also assists other medicines to eliminate several other diseases. Its vitamin-rich (especially vitamin C) qualities make it a basic health tonic in Ayurveda.[60]

Nagarjuna's view on the five kinds of sciences—grammar, mathematics, medicine, logic and philosophy—greatly impacted the medical tradition of East Asia, especially China.

Ophthalmology

Nalanda had advanced ophthalmological studies. Xuanzang, Yijing and Amoghavajra copied many texts related to medicine at Nalanda and introduced them to Tang China.

'These texts mention common eye diseases, types of cataracts, pre-surgery caution and care, choosing the day and time of surgery, kind of *salakas* (needle), surgeon, and use of needles, post-operation bandage, treatment and care. In China, the royal records of the Sui dynasty inform those methods of eye care, treatments to cure diseases related to eyes, and surgeries were introduced in China by the Bodhisattva Nagarjuna (Longshu Pusa). The Buddha is mentioned as a mahabhisaja and the analogy of removing the veil of ignorance with the needle of wisdom was used in the medical surgeries. The surgeons by the blessings of the Buddha removed cataracts with the *salaka* (needle). *The Vairocana Sutra* informs us of such kinds of medical practices and related rituals. The medical treatise found from China, Nepal, and Tibet informs us about the rich tradition of ophthalmological studies in the Indian Buddhist monasteries and Nalanda was one of such institutions which imbibed, experimented, and transmitted for the well-being of humanity.'[61]

Alchemy

The Rasaratnakara, composed by Nagarjuna in early centuries CE in Nalanda is considered the first treatise on Indian alchemy. It evolved with the rise of Mahayana and matured with the beginning of the tantric tradition in Buddhism. 'The work elaborates on the methods of thirteen chemical processes and throws light on the purification of the maharasas (great minerals)—Rajavrata (Lapis lazuli), Gandhaka (sulphur), Rasaka (calamine), Dardaa (cinnabar), Makshika (pyrites), Hema (gold), Tara (silver), and Sulva (copper), extraction of the essence of minerals such as Vaikranta (tourmaline), Makshika and Tapya (assortment of the pyrites), and Abhraka (mica), etc.[62]

It also explains the process of making an elixir for longevity by scrubbing mercury with gold in equal proportions in weight and then amalgamating the mixture with sulphur and borax and gently roasting the preparation.

Rasendramangala, a famous work on alchemy, and *Yogasataka*, a medical treatise, are also assigned to Nagarjuna.

Public health

Nalanda had a well equipped hospital for the resident monks, which also provided free medical services to the inhabitants of the surrounding towns and villages or whoever came seeking medical help. It set a tradition of public health by treating one and all, using knowledge to serve humanity. Nalanda's excellence and best practices in medicine, ophthalmology, alchemy and other health sciences were embraced in Tibet, Nepal, China, Korea, Japan, Mongolia and many parts of the world.

Hatha Yoga

The earliest mention of *Hatha yoga* is found in the Buddhist tantric texts of Vajrayana school, which developed at Nalanda Mahavihara, eighth century onwards. The 11th century tantric Buddhist work *Amrtasiddhi* is the earliest substantial text describing Hatha yoga. The Siddhas belonging to Natha Sampradaya such as Matsyendranath and his disciple Gorakhnath, who are considered saints in both the tantric Buddhist and Hindu traditions, are credited with advancing Hatha yoga. Svatmarama complied *Hathayogapradipika* in 15th century CE from earlier Hatha yoga texts of the Siddhas. The evolution of Hatha yoga over centuries led to democratization of yoga, liberating it from religious and ritualistic dimensions and became the cause of its acceptance and popularity across the world.

Religion

The Buddha, even after his enlightenment, preached for forty-five years to ease the suffering of the mankind. The seekers of Nirvana took inspiration from his life particularly from the Jataka stories in which the Buddha took birth as Bodhisattva sacrificing his own life to save others. The life and ideals of the Jesus Christ have a close parallel to it. The scholastic tradition at Nalanda developed by Nagarjuna popularized the view that these Bodhisattvas were at par with the historical the Buddha himself.

Christianity originated in the early first century CE and the first four canonical gospels date towards the end of the first century CE. Several historians believe that there is a real possibility that Buddhism influenced the early development of Christianity.

William Dalrymple writes in *The Golden Road : How Ancient India Transformed the World*:

Some scholars have suggested that the Buddhist monastic movement which flourished in India from the third century BCE could have had some influence on both the Jewish Essenes in the deserts of Judaea, just above the Red Sea, and on the Christian monks who came to dominate the deserts of the Middle East in late antiquity. Egypt, the landing place of Indians heading westwards, was after all where Christian monasticism began. St Antony, traditionally regarded as the first Christian monk, and the founder of the Christian monastic movement, was born in Alexandria and when he began his flight to the desert he retreated to a cave near the Red Sea, not long after the Berenike Buddha was put to worship in the Isis temple further down the coast. Both Alexandria and the shores of the Red Sea were areas where the presence of Buddhist monks was clearly not uncommon: we know from one of his inscriptions that Ashoka sent his mission as far as Cyrene, modern Libya, around 250 BCE. Some link between the two now seems far from improbable.[63]

The sacred Buddhist texts, relics and other paraphernalia brought from Nalanda by the itinerant Buddhist monks over centuries helped in recreating an Indic Buddhist world in China and in Central and East Asia.

Nalanda Tradition of Conflict Resolution

The administration of the Nalanda Mahavihara was carried by the entire body of monks on democratic principles as noted by Yijing, including the annual allocation of rooms to the monks and trail and punishments of any offences. Any dispute among the residents of the Mahavihara was resolved through debate, discussion and dialogue, which became the celebrated Nalanda tradition of resolving conflicts.

8

Many Nalandas: Nalanda's Global Footprint

The Rise of Nalanda

Forlorn under the red earth
buried for centuries
I rise today like a phoenix,
eight hundred years later
from ashes of my burnt books.

I open my arms today to embrace you
whoever you are, from wherever you are
come, walk into my enlightened fold
as once the Buddha and Mahavira did
seeking shelter in my groves.

I remember Xuanzang and Yizing –
the seekers from the East,
I hear the footsteps of Aryabhata
in my ancient compound today
you too come; come as I rise again.

Although Nalanda Mahavihara declined and turned into ruins
in the early fourteenth century, its reputation as a great seat of

learning continued to spread across geographies and its spirit lived on. Jamphel Shonu[1] writes,

'When we think about Nalanda today, we usually imagine ruins of old temples and monasteries. Some may also think about how invaders supposedly destroyed this great cultural centre of ancient India. Although it is true that the physical structures of Nalanda Mahavihara no longer exist, its history didn't really end in 1193. Rather, it continues to have an impact even today in the way that people imagine and practice Buddhism. The knowledge and teachings that originated there are still prevalent through the networks that it has established. For instance, the philosophical traditions established by Nalanda scholars, such as Nagarjuna, Shantarakshita, Shantideva, etc., continue to influence the teachings of contemporary Mahayana and Vajrayana Buddhism. Even in terms of religious practice, there are remnants of Buddhist religious activities that have continued to this day around Nalanda.'

After the excavation of the Nalanda Mahavihara began in the 1860s, a museum was needed to house the precious archaeological artifacts excavated from the site as well as the adjoining areas. As a result, the Nalanda Archaeological Museum was founded in 1917 adjacent to the ruins of Nalanda Mahavihara. It houses copper plates, coins, bronze statues of several Buddhist, Jain and Hindu deities, basalt stone statues of the Buddha, terracotta jars of the first century, and samples of burnt rice dating to the twelfth century CE. The museum has four galleries displaying 350 objects out of 13,463 objects in its collection, most dating from the fifth–twelfth century CE.

Nava Nalanda Mahavihara was founded in 1951 in Nalanda, Bihar, close to the ruins of the Nalanda Mahavihara, by Dr Rajendra Prasad, the first President of India, to revive the glory of the ancient Nalanda Mahavihara as a centre of higher learning in Pali and Buddhism. It became a deemed university in 2006. On 20 November 1951, the foundation stone of the first building was laid with the following engraving: 'Let the rays of the sun of Nalanda rise from the summit of this rock in order to brighten the vernacular (*lok bhasha*) after the passing away of its nights of darkness (period of its obscurity).'[2]

It started functioning as the Magadh Institute of Post-Graduate Studies and Research in Pali and Allied Languages and Buddhist Learning. Bhikshu Jagdish Kashyap, who had embraced Buddhism, was its founding director.

Nava Nalanda Mahavihara offers undergraduate courses in Pali, diplomas in Pali, Tibetan studies and Chinese, post graduate and PhD courses in Pali, philosophy, ancient history and culture and archaeology, Buddhist studies, Sanskrit, Hindi, English and Tibetan studies, and post graduate diplomas in Vipassana and Yoga, and Buddhist heritage and tourism management.

The international spirit of the institute is upheld by eminent scholars of Buddhist studies visiting as guest lecturers and by engaging in faculty exchange programmes with the reputed and established centres of Buddhist learning around the world.

Located right next to the excavated site of the ancient Nalanda ruins, with its focus on Buddhist studies, this initiative is a serious endeavour to revive 'the lost glory and the heritage of ancient Nalanda Mahavihara.' The revival includes a rich library, named after Dr Rajendra Prasad, which houses a collection of over 67,000 books in a two-storey building. Many of these books have been obtained as donations from eminent Buddhist scholars. The library also houses a number of Xylographic Tibetan manuscripts, a complete set of the sacred books of the East, valuable books on psychology, metaphysics, ethics, logic, sociology and cultural anthropology, donations from Myanmar (Burma), Sri Lanka, Thailand, Cambodia, Japan and South Korea of complete sets of the Tripitaka, a complete set of the Chinese–Buddhist text from the People's Republic of China, a complete set of *Kanjur* (the Buddha's recorded teachings) and *Tanjur* (commentaries by great masters on the Buddha's teachings) donated by His Holiness the Dalai Lama, a complete set of the Tibetan Tripitaka (Peking edition) with its catalogue, Derge and Lhasa editions of Kanjur and Derge, as well as S-Nar-thang editions of Tanjur are also invaluable treasures in the library of the Mahavihara. It also houses a collection of rare manuscripts.

Associated with Nava Nalanda Mahavihara, Xuanzang Memorial Hall is intended to contain relics of the Chinese pilgrim whose gift was negotiated by Nava Nalanda Mahavihara's founding director Jagdish Kashyap with the help of Prime Minister Pandit Jawaharlal Nehru and the erstwhile Chinese Premier Zhou Enlai. The construction, which started in 1957, was completed in 1984. It symbolizes the heritage of Nalanda, thereby strengthening cultural ties between India and China.

Karma Shri Nalanda Institute was founded in 1981 in Sikkim and officially recognised in 1984 by the government of Sikkim, India.

Buddhist sites such as Bodhgaya, Lumbini and Sarnath have monasteries established by Buddhist monks from Southeast and East Asia in line with the Nalanda tradition.

Nalanda Open University was established in 1987 by an ordinance promulgated by the Government of Bihar, later, Nalanda Open University Act, 1995, was passed by the Bihar Legislative Assembly, replacing the ordinance. It provides distance education to applicants on a range of bachelor's and master's degree programmes. In the true spirit of Nalanda Mahavihara, the university offers education to anyone, irrespective of their age, profession, geographical location or economic background.

Dr A.P.J. Abdul Kalam, the former President of India, proposed the revival of the ancient Nalanda Mahavihara while addressing a joint session of the Bihar State Legislative Assembly in 2006. In January 2007, at the Second East Asia Summit in the Philippines, the Singapore government as well as the leaders of sixteen member states of the East Asia Summit (EAS) supported the idea. At the fourth East Asia Summit in October 2009 in Thailand, member states promised further support. Nalanda University Act, 2010 was passed by both houses of the Parliament of India. It became fully functional in September 2014, with the first batch of students. The State Government of Bihar allocated 455 acres of land to the west of Rajgir for the university campus. In 2017, the construction began based on an eco-friendly architecture plan developed by B.V. Doshi, incorporating the elements of the vastu of ancient Nalanda. With a net zero carbon footprint, the Nalanda University campus is the first of its kind in the world built on the principles of sustainability.

Grand in vision, with a diversified curriculum 'the University presently offers programmes in Historical Studies, Ecology and Environment Studies, Buddhist Studies, Philosophy and Comparative Religions, Languages and Literature, Humanities and Management Studies. The programmes offered include Global PhD programme, Masters in Historical Studies (MA), Masters in Ecology and Environment Studies (MSc), Masters in Buddhist Studies, Philosophy and Comparative Religions (MA), Masters in Hindu Studies (MA), Masters in World Literature (MA), Masters in Sustainable Development and Management (MBA), and various short-term diploma and certificate programmes in Pali, Sanskrit, English, Korean, and Yoga'[3] It has an international faculty, international students and international financial support.

It is not a mere attempt to revive ancient Nalanda but, rather, to 'contain within it a memory of the ancient Nalanda University'. It functions under the supervision of the Ministry of External Affairs of India, with initial funding from the governments and individual citizens of several countries.

Along with India, there are seventeen participant countries in this endeavour.

The new campus of the Nalanda University was inaugurated by Prime Minister Narendra Modi in June 2024. On this occasion, he also planted a sapling of the Bodhi tree—an enduring symbol of Buddhist heritage of Indian spirituality at the campus. Ambassadors of seventeen countries (Australia, Bangladesh, Bhutan, Brunei Darussalam, Cambodia, China, Indonesia, Laos, Mauritius, Myanmar, New Zealand, Portugal, Singapore, South Korea, Sri Lanka, Thailand, and Vietnam) were present during the inauguration. During the inauguration PM Modi said— 'Nalanda is not just a renaissance of India's past. The heritage of many countries of the world and Asia is linked to it.'

Nalanda's Global Footprint

Nalanda's fame seems to be growing by the day. Beyond India, Nalanda Mahavihara has inspired the establishment of its namesakes across the world, representing an intriguing continuity of the Mahavihara. It is believed that with the gradual decline of Nalanda and the demise of Buddhism in India, monks left for Nepal and Tibet, where they continued receiving support and patronage and were able to carry on their religious practice. This tradition of naming new institutions after Nalanda Mahavihara suggests continuity of the idea of Nalanda.

A temple called Nalanda Gedige, dating from the eighth–tenth century CE, when Nalanda was still functioning, was

constructed in Sri Lanka. Its structure distinctly resembles a
Pallava style South Indian temple and is considered an attempt
to create a fusion between Hindu Tamil and Buddhist Sinhalese
architectural traditions. A pillar inscription found at the site
tells us that the Buddhist monastery there was originally named
Rajina Vihara and used to host Buddhist monks of the Mahayana
tradition practising tantric Buddhism or Vajrayana. A strict code
of conduct for the residing monks in Sinhalese was found at the
site. It was discovered in 1893 in a deep forest near a village in the
geographical centre of Sri Lanka.

The Great Wild Goose Pagoda, a Nalanda-like tower was
built in Xi'an, China in c.648-649 CE to host the manuscripts
brought back by the Chinese pilgrim Xuanzang. This 210-feet-tall
spectacular sutra library still stands in Xi'an today.

Nalanda is credited by the Tibetan Buddhists as the source of
Tibetan Buddhism and is held in high esteem. Buddhism became the
official religion of Tibet in the eighth century CE, and Shantarakshita,
the head of Nalanda Mahavihara, helped King Trisong Detsen to
establish Tibet's first Buddhist monastery, Samaye.

A Tibetan Nalanda Monastery named Phenpo Nalendra
was founded in 1436 in the Phen-yul valley, to the north-east of
Lhasa, by the monk-scholar Rongton Sheja Kunrig (1347–1449).
It generally had approximately seven hundred resident monks and
thousands of visiting monks. It continues to function and has
branches in various parts of Tibet.

'Named after that incomparable centre of classical Buddhist
learning (Nalendra Monastery in Bihar, India), during its first
twenty years Nalendra grew to house 3,000 monks. 'Rgyun gyi
dbang po' (the Tibetan word for Nalendra) means "the river of
power" and describes well that over the course of more than
500 years, Phenpo Nalendra came to be one of the greatest
Sakya Shedras (colleges) in U district of central Tibet...as a

stronghold of the esoteric practice lineage within the Sakya tradition, Nalendra became the principal monastery of the Tsarpa branch, due to the extraordinary masters of the practice lineage who were its throne holders. It was also a repository of the teachings of all the eight great practice lineages of Tibet and thus was a centre of the broader, non-sectarian approach to Buddhist practice.'[4]

A Nalanda Monastery was founded at Lavaur, about 40 kilometers from Toulouse, France, in 1981, by Lama Zopa Rinpoche and Lama Thubten Yeshe. The land for the monastery was acquired by Elizabeth Drukier, the erstwhile director of the Institut Vajra Yogini, which is also located nearby. It offers basic and masters-degree courses on Mahayana Buddhism. A similar monastery called Institut Tibétan Nalanda is in Brussels.

Nalanda Institute for Contemplative Science was founded in the United States of America by a psychiatrist in 1998 as the Center for Meditation and Healing at the Columbia University Medical Center Department of Psychiatry in New York City with an aim to integrate meditation and yoga with Western health sciences and health education. It is affiliated with the Centre of Buddhist studies, Columbia University and Centre for Complementary and Integrative Medicine at Cornell Medical College.

In 1989, Nalanda Buddhist Centre, Brazil, was created as a tribute to Nalanda Mahavihara. It tried to follow the practices of the original monastery. In 1999, Nalandarama Retreat Centre, Brazil became the first Theravada centre in South America to provide forest-based incentive meditation.

Nalanda College of Buddhist Studies founded by Suwanda H.J. Sugunasiri in 2000 in Toronto offers undergraduate programmes in Buddhist studies.

The International Buddhist College (IBC), founded in 2000 at Hatyai, the largest city in Southern Thailand in 2000, is built like Nalanda to bring together various Buddhist traditions and to promote better understanding of each other. It offers courses in Pali Buddhist studies. A fully residential University like Nalanda Mahavihara, it houses teachers and students, bhiksus and bhiksunis, in three monasteries viz. the Theravada monastery named Ashoka College, the Chinese monastery named Yijing College and the Tibetan monastery named Atisha College.

Nalanda Institute was founded in 2007 on the southern outskirts of Kuala Lumpur, Malaysia, modelled on Nalanda Mahavihara, to promote Buddhist studies in Malaysia. It provides various certificate and diploma courses as well as short training courses to enhance leadership and management skills for Buddhist volunteers on gratis basis and also conducts conferences, symposiums, educational tours, pilgrimage and Buddhist publications.

Nalanda-Sriwijaya Centre was started in 2009 at at the ISEAS —Yusof Ishak Institute, Singapore, 'to develop the 'Nalanda idea' for building a contemporary Asia based on an appreciation of Asian achievements and mutual learning, as exemplified by the cosmopolitan Buddhist centre of learning in Nalanda, as well as the 'Sriwijaya idea' of Southeast Asia as a place of mediation and linkages among the great civilisations.'[5]

Nalanda Institute was established by Abbot, Venerable Thich Linh Tan in 2012 in London to practice Buddhism. Later in 2014, he opened Nalanda Institute Australia in Melbourne to practice Buddhism through meditation, teachings, chanting and celebrating Buddhist festivals.

As evident from the above examples, Nalanda's footprints seem to be spreading to new territories in the twenty-first century, where they have not been strong before.

As our planet faces the triple threats of climate change, biodiversity loss and environmental pollution, humanity needs to make peace, both with its inner self as well as with the fellow species, rivers and lakes, oceans and all entities that support life on our beautiful planet. Nalanda's timeless tradition of imparting knowledge, wisdom, and kindness can guide humanity toward overcoming hatred, anger, frustration, and greed, while fostering inner and outer peace.

The establishment of institutions named after Nalanda inspired by the original Nalanda Mahavihara, across the globe, gives me hope that humanity would someday learn to settle all its disputes through the great Nalanda tradition of debate, discussion and dialogue and abhor violence and war forever. In this direction Nalanda's continuity and resurgence within India and abroad is a source of great hope.

Acknowledgements

I'm grateful to Dhanya Madhvan Nair for her valuable insights and research inputs, constant support and encouragement in writing this book. I thank Chaitali Pandya for reading the manuscript and providing her feedback. I would like to thank Milee Ashwarya, publisher, Penguin Random House, India for commissioning this timely book.

Bibliography

Adikaram, F.W, Bary. *History of Buddhism in Ceylon, Colombo*: Buddhist Cultural Centre, 2009.

Agrawala, V.S and Krishna Deva, *The Stone Temple of Nalanda*, Journal of UP Historical Society, vol. 23, 1950.

Alice Getty, *The Gods of Northern Buddhism (Reprint)*, Tokyo: Charles E. Tuttle Co, 1962.

Allchin, F.R, Erdosy George. The Archaeology of Early Historic South Asia: The Emergence of Cities and States. Cambridge University Press (1995)

Almond, P.C., *The British Discovery of Buddhism*, Cambridge: Cambridge University Press, 1988.

Altekar, A.S. and V. Mishra, *Report on Kumrahar Excavation*, 1951-55, Patna: K.P. Jayaswal Research Institute, 1959.

Altekar. A. S, *Introduction of the General Editor in Biography of Dharmasvamin*, tr. George Roerich, Patna: K.P. Jayaswal, 2016.

Arunasir,'Nalanda-2', *Encyclopedia of Buddhism, vol. VII, Fascicle, I*, Colombo: Department of Buddhist Affairs, 2003.

Asher, Frederick M, Nalanda: Situating the Great Monastery, Mumbai, Marg. Foundation, 2015.

Asher, Frederick, India, Magadha, *Nalanda: Ecology and a PreModern World System*, in Records, Recoveries, Remnants, and Inter-Asian Interconnections, Decoding Cultural Heritage, ed. Anjana Sharma, Singapore: ISEAS Publishing, 2018.

Bagchi, Prabodh Chandra. *India and China: A Thousand Years of Cultural Relations.* New Delhi, 2008.

Bailey, Greg, and Ian Mabbet. *The Sociology of Early Buddhism.* Cambridge: Cambridge University Press, 2003.

Banerjea, Jitendra Nath, The Development of Hindu Iconography, Calcutta, 1956.

Banerji, R.D., Eastern Indian School of Medieval Sculpture, Delhi: Manager of Publications, 1933.

Barth, Auguste. *The Religions of India.* London: Trübner & Co., 1822.

Barua, Benimadhab. *Gayà and Bodhgaya.* Calcutta: Indian Research Institute, 1934.

Basham, A. L. *History and Doctrine of the Aperkas: A Vanished Indian Religion.* London: Luzac and Company, 1951.

Basham, A. L. *The Wonder That Was India.* New Delhi, 1967.

Bapat, P.V. (ed), 2500 years of Buddhism, New Delhi: Govt. of India, Publication Division, 1987.

Barlingay, S.S.: A Modern Introduction to Indian Logic, National Publishing House, Delhi,1976.

Barua, D.K, Viharas in Ancient India: A Survey of Buddhist Monasteries, Calcutta: Indian Publications Monograph Series No. 10, 1969.

Basu, Durga. 'Stucco as a Building Material: A Study of Its Composition, Use and Scientific Analysis.' *Heritage: Journal of Multidisciplinary Studies in Archaeology*, vol. 8, no. 2, 2020.

Beal, S, Buddhist Records of the Western World (by Hiuen Tsang), 2 vols, London, 1906. (trans.)

Beal, S. *The Life of Hiuen-Tsiang by the Shaman Hwui Li, with an Introduction Containing an Account of the Works of I-Tsing.* London, 1911. Reprint: New Delhi: Munshiram Manoharlal, 1973.

Beal, S. *St-Yu-Ki: Buddhist Record of the Western World, Part III.* 1906. Translated from the Chinese of Hiuen-Tsang (AD 629). London: Trübner, 1984. Reprint ed.: Delhi, 1969.

Beckwith, Christopher I. *Warriors of the Cloisters.* Princeton: Princeton University Press, 2012.

Bellina, Bérénice. 'Beads, Social Change and Interaction Between India and South-East Asia.' *Antiquity,* 2003.

Berkwitz, Stephen C., Juliane Schober, and Claudia Brown. 'Introduction: Rethinking Buddhist Manuscript Cultures.' In *Buddhist Manuscript Cultures: Knowledge, Ritual, and Art,* edited by Stephen C. Berkwitz, Juliane Schober, and Claudia Brown. London and New York: Routledge, 2009.

Bernet, A. J. Kempers. *The Bronzes of Nalanda and Hindu Javanese Art.* Leiden, 1993.

Bhattacharya, Binortos. *An Introduction to Buddhist Esoterism.* Bombay: Oxford University Press, 1932.

Bhattacharya, Benoy Gosh. *The Indian Buddhist Iconography.* Calcutta: K.L. Mukhopadhyay, 1958.

Bhattacharya, Benoy Gosh. *Nispannayogavali of Mahapandita Abhayakaragupta.* Baroda: Oriental Institute.

Bhattacharya, P. N. 'Nalanda Plate of Dharmapaladeva.' *Epigraphia Indica,* vol. XXIII, 1935-36.

Bhattacharya, D. C. *Iconology of Composite Images.* Delhi, 1980.

Bhattacharya, D. C. *Studies in Buddhist Iconography.* Delhi: Manohar Publishers, 1978.

Bhattacharya, D. C. *Tantric Buddhist Iconography Sources.* New Delhi: Munshiram Manoharlal, 1974.

Bhattacharya, Kamaleswar, E. H. Johnston, and Arnold Kunst. *The Dialectical Method of Nāgārjuna.* Delhi: Motilal Banarsidass, 1978.

Bhattasali, N. K. *Iconography of Buddhist and Brahmanical Sculptures in the Dacca Museum.* Dacca Museum Committee, 1929.

Bigandet, Paul. *The Life or Legend of Gaudama, the Buddha of the Burmese,* vol. 1. London: Kegan Paul, Trench, Trubner & Co., 1911-12.

Birnbaum, Raoul. *The Healing the Buddha.* Boston: Shambala, 1989.

Bloss, Lowell W. 'The Buddha and the Naga: A Study in Buddhist Folk Religiosity.' *History of Religions,* 1973.

Bodhi, Bhikkhu. *The Connected Discovery of the Buddha.* Boston: Wisdom Publications, 2000.

Bose, Kurethara S. 'The Transformation of Self in Mahayana Buddhism: A Theoretical Study.' *The Eastern Buddhist,* vol. 27, no. 2, 1994.

Bose, Phanindra Nath. *The Indian Teachers in China.* Madras: S. Ganesan, 1923.

Boucher, Daniel. 'The Pratityasamutpada Gatha and Its Role in the Medieval Cult of the Relics.' *The Journal of the International Association of Buddhist Studies,* vol. 14, no. 1, 1991.

Bronkhorst, Johannes. *Buddhist Teaching in India.* Boston, 2009.

Bronkhorst, Johannes. *Buddhism in the Shadow of Brahmanism.* Leiden, 2011.

Bronson, B., and G. F. Dales. 'Excavation at Hansen, Thailand, 1968 and 1969: A Preliminary Report.' *Asian Perspectives,* 1972.

Brose, Benjamin. *Xuanzang: China's Legendary Pilgrim and Translator.* Boulder, Colo., 2021.

Buddhist Monastic Traditions of Southern Asia: A Record of the Inner Law Sent from the South Seas, translated by Li Rongxi. Berkeley, 2000.

Brown, Percy. *Indian Architecture (Buddhist and Hindu Period),* Bombay

Brown, Robert. 'Bodhgaya and Southeast Asia.' In *Bodhgaya: The Site of Enlightenment,* edited by Janice Leoshko. Bombay: Marg Publications, 1988.

Buchanan, Francis. *An Account of Districts of Bihar and Patna in 1811-12,* vol. 1. Patna: Bihar and Orissa Research Society, 1839.

Burgess, J. *Notes on the Amaravati Stupa.* Madras: Archaeological Survey of India, 1882.

Casparis, J. G. de. 'Expansion of Buddhism into Southeast Asia.' *Ancient Ceylon,* 1990.

Chakrabarti, Dilip K., Ajit K. Prasad, S. K. Prasad, K. Anand, and P. K. Chattopadhyay. 'Preliminary Observations on the Distribution of Archaeological Sites in the South Bihar Plain.' *South Asian Studies,* 1995.

Chakravarti, N.P., Two Brick Inscriptions of Nalandā', Epigraphia Indica, vol. XXI, 1931-32

Chakravarti, N., Pala Inscription in the Indian Museum', JPASB IV 1908

Chemburkar, Swati. 'Visualizing the Buddhist Mandala: Kesariya, Borobudur and Tabo.' In *India and Southeast Asia: Cultural Discourses,* edited by Anna L. Dallapiccola and Anila Verghese. Mumbai, 2017.

Chemburkar, Swati, and Andrea Acri, eds. 'Borobudur's Pāla Forbear? A Field Note from Kesariya, Bihar, India.' In *Esoteric Buddhism in Medieval Maritime Asia: Networks of Masters, Texts, Icons.* ISEAS–Yusof Ishak Institute.

Ch'en, Mei-Chin. The Eminent Chinese Monk Hsuan-Tsang: His Contributions to Buddhist Scripture Translation and to the Propagation of Buddhism in China. Ph.D. dissertation, University of Wisconsin, Madison.1992.

Chi, R.S.Y, Buddhist Formal Logic: A study of Dignaga's Hetucakara and K'eui-Ci's

Chemburkar, Swati. 'Stupa to Mandala: Tracing a Buddhist Architectural Development from Kesaria to Borobudur to Tabo.' *Pacific World,* Third Series, no. 20, 2018.

Chemburkar, Swati. 'Stupa to Mandala: Tracing a Buddhist Architectural Development from Kesaria to Borobudur to Tabo.' Pacific World, Third Series, no. 20, 2018.

Chhabra, Bahadurchand, and G. S. Gai. *Corpus Inscriptionum Indicarum*, vol. III. New Delhi: Archaeological Survey of India, 1981.

Clough, Bradley S. 'The Higher Knowledge in the Pali Nikayas and Vinaya.' *Journal of the International Association of Buddhist Studies,* vol. 33, 2010.

Conze, Edward. *The Perfection of Wisdom in Eight Thousand Lives and Its Verse Summary.* Delhi: Sri Satguru, 1994.

Conze, Edward. *Thirty Years of Buddhist Studies: Selected Essays.* Oxford: Bruno Cassirer, 1967.

Coomaraswamy, Ananda K. 'The Origin of the Buddha Image.' *The Art Bulletin,* 1927.

Cox, Collett. Disputed Dharmas: Early Buddhist Theories on Existence. An Annotated Translation of the Section on Factors Dissociated from Thought from Sanoghabhadra's Nyāyānusāra. Tokyo: International Institute for Buddhist Studies.1995.

Cunningham, A., Ancient Geography of India (eds) S.N Majumdar and M.N Sastri, Calcutta, 1924.

Dalrymple, William: The Golden Road, Bloomsbury, 2024.

Darian, Steven. 'Buddhism in Bihar from Eighth to the Twelfth Century with Special Reference to Nalanda.' *Asiatische Studien/Études Asiatiques,* vol. 25, 1971.

Datta, and Chatterjee, S. C. *An Introduction to Indian Philosophy.* University of Calcutta, Calcutta, 6th ed., 1960.

Das, S. R. *Rajbadidanga.* Kolkata: Asiatic Society, 1962.

Dasgupta, S. N. *A History of Indian Philosophy,* 5 vols. Cambridge: Cambridge University Press, 1957.

Datta, Bhupendranath. *Mystic Tales of Lama Taranatha: A Religio-Sociological History of Mahayana Buddhism.* Calcutta: Ramkrishna Vedanta Matha, 1944.

Davids, Rhys W. *Buddhism: Its History and Literature.* Calcutta, 1952.

Dessein, Bart. 'The Mahasanghikas and the Origin of Mahayana Buddhism: Evidence Provided in the *Abhdharmamaha-vibhasasastra.' The Eastern Buddhist,* 2009.

Devahuti, D. *The Unknown Huan-Tsang.* New Delhi: Oxford University Press, 2001.

Dhavalikar, M. K. 'The Origin of Tara.' *Bulletin of the Deccan College Post-Graduate and Research Institute,* 1963–64.

Dutt, Nalinaksha, Buddhist Sects in India (Reprint), Delhi: Motilal Banarsidass, 1998.

Dutt, S., Early Buddhist Monachism (600 BC to 100 A.D), London, 1924.

Dutt, Sukumar, Buddhist Monks and Monasteries of India: Their History and their Contribution to Indian Culture. London: George Alllen & Unwin Ltd.; (first edition), 1962.

Dziwenka, Ronald James. "'The Last Light of Indian Buddhism'— The Monk Zhikong in 14th Century China and Korea." PhD dissertation, The University of Arizona, 2010.

Elliot, H. M., and John Dowson. *The History of India as Told by its Own Historians,* vols. I and II. New Delhi: Low Price Publishers, 1996.

Fergusson, James. *Tree and Serpent Worship or Illustrations of Mythology and Art in India in the First and Fourth Centuries after Christ from the Sculptures of Buddhist Topes at Sanchi and Amaravati.* New Delhi: Asian Educational Services, 2001.

Fickeler, P. 'Fundamental Questions in the Geography of Religion.' In *Readings in Cultural Geography,* edited by M. Mikesell and P. Wagner. Chicago, 1962.

Findly, E. B. *Dana: Giving and Getting in Pali Buddhism.* Delhi: Motilal Banarsidass, 2003.

Ganvir, Shrikant. 'Cultural Linkage between Ancient Buddhist Art of India and East: A Case Study of Eleven-Headed Avalokitesvara.' *Bulletin of the Deccan College Post-Graduate and Research Institute,* vol. 72–73, 2012–13.

Ganvir, Srikant. 'Representation of Naga in Buddhist Art of Amaravati: A Sculptural Analysis.' *Proceedings of the Indian History Congress,* 2010–11.

Getty, Alice. *The Gods of Northern Buddhism.* Tokyo: Charles E. Turtle Company, 1962.

Ghosh, Amalananda. 'Nalanda Plate of Samudragupta: The Year 5.' *Epigraphia Indica,* vol. XXV, 1939–40.

Ghosh, A. 'A Bronze Image Inscription from Nalanda.' *Epigraphia Indica,* vol. XXV, 1939–40.

Ghosh, Mallar. *Development of Buddhist Iconography in Eastern India: A Study of Tara, Prañas of Five Tathagatas and Bhrkuti.* New Delhi: Munshiram Manoharlal, 1980.

Glower, I. C. 'The Role of India in the Late Prehistory of Southeast Asia.' *Journal of South-East Asian Archaeology,* 1998.

Goodrich, L. C. 'The Revolving Book-Case in China.' *Harvard Journal of Asiatic Studies,* vol. 7, 1942–43.

Goyal, S. R. *The Imperial Guptas: A Multidisciplinary Political Study.* Meerut: Kushmanjali Publication, 2005.

Gupta, P.L., Patna Museum Catalogue of Antiquities, Patna, 1965.

Guy, John (ed.). *Lost Kingdoms: Hindu-Buddhist Sculpture of Early Southeast Asia.* New York, 2014.

Grunwedel, Albert. *Buddhist Art in India.* London: B. Quaritch Collection, 1901.

Habib, Irfan. 'Medieval Popular Monotheism and its Humanism: The Historical Settings.' *Social Scientist,* vol. 21, nos. 3–4, March–April 1996.

Heras, M., The Royal Patrons of the University of Nalanda',
JBORS XIV, 1928.

Hirakawa, Akira. A History of Indian Buddhism: from Śākyamuni
to Early Mahāyāna. Trans. Paul Groner. Honolulu: University
of Hawaii Press. 1990

Huntington, Susan L, The 'Pala-Sena' Schools of Sculpture,
Leiden: E.J. Brill, 1984.

Hoernle, A. E. Rudolf. *Studies in the Medicine of Ancient India.*
Oxford: The Clarendon Press, 1907.

Huntington, Susan L. *The 'Pala-Sena' School of Sculpture.* Leiden:
E. J. Brill, 1984.

Hyecho, Jan Yun-Hua, Lida Shotaro, Yang Han-Sung, and
Laurence Preston. *The Hye Ch'o Diary: Memoir of the
Pilgrimage to the Five Regions of India.* New Delhi: Asian
Humanities Press, 1984.

Ichimura, Shohei. 'Reexamining the Period of Nagarjuna: Western
India AD 50–150.' *Journal of Indian and Buddhist Studies,*
vol. 40, no. 2, 1992.

Ingalls, D..H..H..: Materials for the Study of Navyanyaya Logic,
Harvard Oriental Series, No. 40, Harvard University press,
Cambridge, Mass,1951.

James, E. O. *The Cult of the Mother Goddess: An Archaeological and
Documentary Study.* California: The Book Tree, 2018.

Jayaswal, Vidula. *Kushana Clay Art of Ganga Plains: A Case
Study of Human Forms from Khairadih.* Delhi: Agam Kala
Prakashan, 1991.

Jayaswal, Vidula. *Buddhacarita or Acts of the Buddha* (original
work by Asvaghosa). Blue Dove Press, 1998.

Kane, P. V. *History of Dharmasastra*, vols. II & III. Poona:
Bhandarkar Research Institute, 1993.

Kalupahana, David. *Mulamadhyamakakarika of Nagarjuna* (Reprint). Delhi: Motilal Banarsidass Publishers, 1999.

Keira, Ryusei. Madhyamaka and Epistemology: A Study of Kamalaśīla's Method for Proving the Voidness of All Dharmas. Vienna: Arbeitskreis für Tibetische und Buddhistische Studien, Universität Wien. 2004

Kenn, H. Manual of Indian Buddhism: New Impression,ed by C.Mani, Delhi: Bharatiya Kala Prakashan, 1995. (trans.), Saddharmapundarika-sutra (The Lots Sutra of the True Law), Kessinger, 2003.

Kenoyer, Jonathan Mark. *Ancient Cities of the Indus Valley Civilization.* New York: Oxford University Press, 1998.

Kempers, A.J.B, The Bronzes of Nalanda and Hindu-Javanese Art, Leiden, 1933.

Kim, Jinah. 'A Book of Buddhist Goddesses: Illustrated Manuscripts of the "Pañcaraksa Sutra" and Their Ritual Use'. *Artibus Asiae*, 2010.

Kumar, Brajmohan, Archaeology of Pataliputra and Nalanda, Delhi: Ramanand Vidya Bhawan, 1987.

Kuraishi, M.H, Excavations of Nalanda, ASI, A.R, 1929-30, Delhi 1935. A Short Guide to the Buddhist Remains Excavated at Nalanda, Calcutta: Govt of India, 1970

Kumar, Vijay, and Alok Ranjan. 'Seals and Sealings Kept at Nalanda Archaeological Museum, Nalanda District, Bihar'. *Indian Journal of Archaeology*, vol. 7, no. 2, 2022.

Kuraishi, M.H., and G.C. Chandra. *Excavations of Nalanda*, ASI, A.R. Pt-II, 1930-34.

Krishnamurthy, S., and K.C. Srivastava. 'A Study of Some Sealings from Rukministhan Excavation, District Nalanda, Bihar'. In *Art, Archaeology and Museology*, ed. Dilip Kumar. New Delhi: B.R. Publications, 2020.

Kritzer, Robert. Vasubandhu and the Yogācārabhūmi: Yogācāra Elements in the Abihidharmakośabhāsya. Tokyo: International Institute for Buddhist Studies.2005

Lahri, Latika. *I-Ching: Chinese Monk in India: Biography of Eminent Monks Who Went to the Western World in Search of Law During the Great Tang Dynasty.* Delhi: Motilal Banarsidass, 1986.

Lal, B.B. 'An Examination of Some Metal Images from Nalanda, Ancient India'. *Bulletin of Archaeological Survey of India*, no. 12, 1956.

Lama Chimpa and Alaka Chattopadhyay (trans), Tananatha's History of Buddhism, New Delhi, Motilal Banarsidass publishers, 1970.

Lamotte, Etienne. *History of Indian Buddhism: From the Origins to the Saka Era.* Paris: L'Institut Orientaliste De Louvain, 1988.

Latika, Lahiri, Chinese Monks in India by I- Ching, New Delhi, Motilal Banarsidass Publishers Pvt.Ltd. 1986

Law, B.C., Geography of Early Buddhism, London, 1927.

Law, B.C. *Historical Geography of Ancient India.* New Delhi: Munshiram Manoharlal, 2016.

Law, B.C. "Formulation of Pratityasamutpada." *The Journal of the Royal Asiatic Society of Great Britain and Ireland*, no. 2, 1937.

Lee, Kw Angsu. "Trade and Religious Contacts between India and Korea in Ancient Times." *Proceedings of Indian History Congress*, vol. 54, 1993.

Legge, J., Travels of Fa-hein, Oxford, 1816.

Legge, James (trans)., A Record of Buddhist Kingdom: Being an Account by the Chinese Monk Fa-hein of His Travels in India and Ceylon (AD 399-414) in Search of the Buddhist Books of Discipline, Oxford: Clarendon Press, 1986.

Leighton, Taigen Daniel. *Faces of Compassion: Classic Bodhisattva Archetypes and Their Modern Expression.* Boston: Wisdom Publications, 2003.

Leoshko, Jenice. "The Vajrasana Buddha." *Visions of Enlightenment: The Heritage of Bodh Gaya*, vol. VXXXX, no. 1, 1988.

Levi, S. (ed.). *Mahayana Sutralankara of Asanga*, Vol. I. Paris, 1907.

Li, Shaman Hwui. *The Life of Hiuen-Tsiang*, trans. Samuel Beal. London, 1911.

Liu, Xinru. *Ancient India and Ancient China: Trade and Religious Exchange AD 1-600*. Oxford, 1988.

Loizzo, J.J. *Candrakīrti and the Moonflower of Nālandā: Objectivity and Self-Correction in the Buddhist Central Philosophy of Language*. Columbia University, 2001.

Lopez, Jr., Donald. *Hye Cho's Journey: The World of Buddhism*. Chicago: The University of Chicago Press, 2017.

Longhurst, A.H. *The Buddhist Antiquities of Nagarjunakonda, Madras Presidency*. Memoirs of Archaeological Survey of India, no. 54. New Delhi: Archaeological Survey of India, 1999.

Lowe, Roy, and Yasuhara, Yoshihito. *The Origins of Higher Learning: Knowledge Networks and the Early Development of Universities*. London, 2017.

Mabbet, I.W. "The 'Indianization' of Southeast Asia: Reflections on Historical Sources." *Journal of Southeast Asian Studies*, vol. 8, 1977.

Mahalingana, T.V. *The Nagas in Indian History and Culture*. Madras: G.S. Press, 1965.

Maheshwari, Madhurika K. *From Ogress to Goddess, Hariti, A Buddhist Deity*. Mumbai: IIRNS Publications, 2009.

Maity, S.K. *The Imperial Guptas and Their Times*. Delhi: Munshiram Manoharlal, 1975.

Majumdar, N.G., 'Nalanda Inscription of Vipulasrimitra', EI XXI, 3 July 1931.

Majumdar, N.G. "Nalanda Inscription of Vipulasrimitra." *Epigraphia Indica*, vol. XXI, 1931-32.

Majumdar, R.C. *Hindu Colonies in the Far East*. Calcutta: Firma.

Mukhopadhyay, K.L., ed. *The Age of Imperial Kannauj*. Bombay: Vidya Bhavan, 1993.

Makdisi, George. "On the Origin and Development of the College in Islam and the West." In *Islam and the Medieval West: Aspects of Intercultural Relations*, edited by Khalil I. Semaan, Albany, NY, 1980.

Malalasekera, G.P. *Dictionary of Pali Proper Names*, 2 vols. New Delhi: Motilal Banarsidass, 2007.

Mall, Linnart. *Studies in the Aṣṭasahastikā Prajñāpāramitā and Other Essays*. Delhi: Motilal Banarsidass, 2005.

Mani, B.R., The Kushan Civilization, New Delhi: D.K. Printers, 1985.

Mani, C. (ed.), The Social Philosophy of Buddhism, Sarnath: Central Institute of Higher Tibetan Studies, 1972.

Mani, C (ed.) The Heritage of Nalanda, New Delhi, Aryan Books international, 2008

Marasinghe, E.W., The Vasturidyasastra Ascribed to Manjusri, New Delhi: Sri Satguru Publications, 1989.

Matilal, B.K.: The Navya-Nyaya Doctrine of Negation, Harvard Oriental Series No. 46, Harvard University Press, Cambridge, Mass, 1968.

Marshall, John. *Taxila: An Illustrated Account of Archaeological Excavations Carried Out at Taxila under the Orders of the Government of India Between the Years 1913 and 1934*, 3 vols. Cambridge: Cambridge University Press, 1951.

Matsunaga, Daigan, and Alicia Matsunaga. "The Concept of Upaya in Mahayana Buddhist Philosophy." *Japanese Journal of Religious Studies*, 1974.

Miller, Roy Andrew. *The Footprints of the Buddha: An Eighth Century Old Japanese Poetic Sequence*. New York: American Oriental Society, 1975.

Mufti, T.R.V.: The Central Philosophy of Buddhism. George Allend & Unwin Ltd. London (2nd ed.) 1968.

Mishra, B.N. 'Architecture of the Nalanda Monasteries', in *Ratna-chandrica: Panorama of Oriental Studies*, ed. Devendra Handa and Ashvini Agrawal, Jaipur: Harman Publication, 1989.

Mishra, B.N., Nalanda (3 vols.), Delhi: B.R. Publishing Corporation, 1989.

Mishra, P.K., Nikoshey, J.K., Tewari, Abdul Arif, Neetesh Saxena, Dhanajay Kumar, S.P. Gupta, and O.P. Pandey, 'Excavation at Begumpur, District Nalanda', *Indian Archaeology: A Review*, 2007-8.

Mishra, Vüaykanta, 'A New Sanskrit Prasasti from Nalanda', *The Journal of Bihar Research Society*, vol. LVII (I-IV), 1972.

Mishra, V.D., *Some Aspects of Indian Archaeology*, Allahabad: Prabhat Prakashan, 1977.

Mishra, V.A., 'The Mesolithic Age in India', in *Prehistory: Archaeology of South Asia*, ed. S. Settar and Ravi Korisettar, Delhi: Manohar, 2002.

Mitra, Devala, 'Iconographical Notes', *Journal of Asiatic Society*, vol. 1, no. 1, 1959.

Mitra, Debala, Buddhist Monuments, Calcutta: Sahitya Samsad, 1971.

Mitra, R.I., 'A Buddhist Inscription from Bodhgaya of the Reign of Jayachandradeva', *Proceedings of Asiatic Society of Bengal*, Calcutta, 1880.

Mitra, R.L., Buddha-Gaya: The Hermitage of Sakyamuni, Calcutta: The Bengal Secretariat Press, 1878, reprinted Delhi, Varanasi: Indological Book House, 1972.

Mitra, Sisir, K. (ed.), East Indian Bronzes, Calcutta: Centre of Advanced Study in Ancient Indian History and Culture. Calcutta University, 1979.

Mohanty, Bimlendu, *Buddhist Heritage of Orissa (From Kalinga to Sri Lanka)*, New Delhi: Vohra Publications, 2009.

Mookerji, Radha Kumud, *Ancient Indian Education, Brahmanical and Buddhist*, New Delhi: Motilal Banarsidass, 2003.

Mookerjee, S., Buddhist Philosophy of Universal Flux, New Delhi: Motilal Banarsidass, 1975.

Mukherji, P.C., *Report on Tour of Exploration of the Antiquities in Tarai, Nepal, The Region of Kapilvastu During February and March 1899*, Calcutta: Office of the Superintendent of Government Printing, 1901.

Mulin, Glenn H., *Readings on the Six Yogas of Naropa*, New York: Snow Lion, 1977.

Nakamura, Hajime, *Indian Buddhism: A Survey of Bibliographical Notes*, Delhi: Motilal Banarsidass, 1986.

Narain, H.K., B. Nath, and Sunil Kumar, *Excavation at Nalanda, District Nalanda*, Indian Archaeology, 1981-82.

Narayan, H.K., B. Nath, Sunil Kumar, and Indu Prakash, *Excavation at Nalanda, District Nalanda*, Indian Archaeology, 1982-83.

Nath Prasad, Birendra, *A 'Nālandā Monk' in the Late Thirteenth–Early Fourteenth Century India, Tibet, China and Korea: A Note on the 'Poetic Inscription' on a Korean Stūpa Erected in the Memory of Dhyānabhadra*, Routledge, 2021.

Nichols, S.G., 'Introduction: Philology in a Manuscript Culture', *Speculum*, 1990.

Nomination Dossier: Property: Excavated Remains of Nalanda Mahavihara, UNESCO World Heritage Centre, 2016.

O'Connor, S.J. and T. Harrison, 'Gold Foiled Amulets in Bali, Philippines, and Borneo', *Journal of the Malaysian Branch of the Royal Asiatic Society*, vol. 44, 1977.

Obeyesekere, Ranjini, *Yasodhara, The Wife of the Bodhisatta*, Albany: State University of New York Press, 2009.

Oldham, C.E., *The Sun and Serpent: A Contribution to the History of Serpent Worship*, New Delhi: Gyan Publishing House, 2020.

Pande, G.C.: studies in the Origin of Buddhism. University of Allahabad, Allahabad 1957.

Panth, Dr. R, Nalanda and Buddhism, Nalanda: Nava Nalanda Mahavihara, 2002.

Panth, Rabindra (Editor), Contribution of Nalanda to the World Culture, Bihar, Nava Nalanda Mahavira publishers, 2009

Pargiter, F.E., 'A Copperplate Discovered at Kasia, and the Buddha's Death-Place', *The Journal of the Royal Asiatic Society of Great Britain and Ireland*, 1913.

Pathak, Suniti Kumar, 'A Dharani Mantra in the Vinaya-Vastu', *Bulletin of Tibetology*, no. 2, 1989.

Patil, D.R., *The Antiquarian Remains of Bihar*, Patna: K.P. Jayaswal Research Institute, 1963.

Paul, Debajani, *The Art of Nalanda: Development of Buddhist Sculpture AD 600-1200*, Delhi: Munshiram Manoharlal, 1995.

Paz, Octavio, In Light of India, (trans) Eliot Weinberger, New York, Harcourt Brace and Company. 1997.

Possehl, Gregory L., *The Indus Civilization, A Contemporary Perspective*, Delhi: Vistar Publications, 2012.

Prabhavananda, Svami, *The Spiritual Heritage of India: A Clear Summary of Indian Philosophy and Religion*, Madras: Vedanta Publisher, 1977.

Prasad, Chandra Shekhar, 'Nalanda vis-à-vis the Birthplace of Shariputra', *East and West*, 1988.

Prebish Charles s. (ed): Historical Dictionary of Buddhism, Sri Satguru Publications, Delhi, 1995.

Prematilleke, Leelananda, 'Ancient Monastic Hospital System in Sri Lanka', in *Ancient Trade and Cultural Contexts in Southeast Asia*, ed. A. Srisuchat, Bangkok: Office of National Cultural Commission, 1996.

Radhakrishnan, S, Indian philosophy, London, G. Allen & Unwin Ltd, 1923.

Rahula, Walpola, *History of Buddhism in Ceylon*, Colombo: Buddhist Cultural Centre, 2014.

Rajpitak, W., *The Development of Copper Alloy Metallurgy in Thailand in Pre-Buddhist Period with Special Reference to High Tin Bronzes*, PhD thesis (unpublished), London: University of London, 1983.

Raju, D.R. and P.C. Venkatasubbaiah, 'The Archaeology of the Upper Paleolithic Phases in India', in *Pre-History: Archaeology of South Asia*, Delhi: Manohar, 2002.

Ramachandran, T.N., *Nagarjunakonda*, Memoirs of Archaeological Survey of India, no. 71, 1938, New Delhi: Archaeological Survey of India, 1999.

Ramanan, V., Nagarjuna's Philosophy, Delhi: Banarsidass, 1975.

Ramesh, K.V., Indian Inscriptions: A Study in Comparison and Contrast, New Delhi: Indian Council of Historical Research, 2006.

Randle, H.N., Fragments from Dinnaga, Delhi: Sundeep Prakashan, 1981.

Rao, K.P., 'Early Trade and Contacts between South India and Southeast Asia (300 BCE-AD 200)', *East and West*, vol. 51, nos. 3-4, 2001.

Ray, Chaudhuri, Hemachandra, Political History of Ancient India (6th edn.). Calcutta, 1953.

Ray, Haraprasad, 'The Identity of Huang-chih: An Ancient Indian Kingdom in Intimate Contacts with Han China', *Indian Historical Review*, vol. XVII, nos. 1-2, 1990.

Ray, P.C., *A History of Hindu Chemistry: From the Earliest Times to the Middle of the Sixteenth Century AD*, New Delhi: Cosmo Publications, 2010.

Raychaudhury, Hemchandra, *Political History of Ancient India*, Calcutta: University of Calcutta, 1972.

Rhys Davids, T.W., *Buddhist Suttas*, SBE, vol. II, New Delhi: Motilal Banarsidass, 1989.

Rhi, Juhyung. "Some Textual Parallels for Gandharan Art: Fasting Buddhas, Lalitavistara, and Karuna Pundarika." *Journal of the International Association of Buddhist Studies*, 2006.

Rinpoche, L. Samdong, and C. Mani, Madhyamika Dialectic and Philosophy of Nagarjuna, Sarnath: Central Institute of Higher Tibetan Studies, 1985.

Robinson, James B., Buddha's Lion: The Lives of the Eighty Four Siddhas, Berkeley: Dharma Publishing, 1979.

Robinson, R.: Early Buddhist theory of Knowledge Philosophy: East and West, Vol. No. 19, (1969)

Roerich, George. Biography of Dhammasvāmī (Chag Lo tsa-baChos- rje-dpal), Patna, K.P. Jayaswal Research Institute, 1959:62-63

Rongxi, Li, trans., *The Great Tang Dynasty Record of the Western Regions*, Berkeley: Numata Center for Translation and Research, 1996.

Ruegg, David Seyfort, "Aspects of the Investigation of the Earlier Indian Mahayana," *Journal of the International Association of Buddhist Studies*, vol. 27, no. 1, 2004.

Ryukan, Kimura, *A Historical Study of the Terms Hinayana and Mahayana and the Origin of Mahayana Buddhism*, Calcutta: University of Calcutta, 1927.

Sahai, Bhagwant, *The Inscriptions of Bihar: From Earliest Times to the Middle of 13th Century AD*, New Delhi: Ramanand Vidya Bhawan, 1983.

Sahu, N.K., *Buddhism in Orissa*, Bhuvaneshvar: Utkal University, 1958.

Salomon, Richard, *Ancient Buddhist Scrolls from Gandhara*, London: The British Library, 1999.

Samaddar, J.N., Glories of Magadha, Patna: K. P. Jayaswal Institute,1990.

Samuels, Jeffrey, 'Towards the Action-Oriented Pedagogy: Buddhist Texts and Monastic Education in Contemporary Sri Lanka', *Journal of American Academy of Religion*, vol. 72, no. 4, 2004.

Sander, L., 'Early Prakrit and Sanskrit Manuscripts from Xinjiang (Second to Fifth/Sixth Centuries CE): Paleography, Literary Evidence, and their Relation to Buddhist Schools', in *Collection of Essays*, 1993.

Sankalia, Hasmukh, University of Nalanda, Madras, B.G. Paul and Publishers. 1934.

Samaddar, J.N., *Glories of Magadha* (2nd edn.), Patna, 1927.

Sasaki, Shizuka, 'The Mahaparinirvana Sütra and the Origin of Mahayana Buddhism', *Japanese Journal of Religious Studies*, vol. 26, nos. 1-2, 1999.

Sastri, Hirananda, *Nalanda and its Epigraphic Material*: Memoirs of the Archaeological Survey of India, Delhi, 1942.

Sastri, Aiyaswami N., *Alambanapariksa and Vritti by Dinnaga with the Commentary of Dharmapāla*, Madras: The Adyar Library, 1942.

Sastri, P.S., 'Nagarjuna and Aryadeva', *Indian Historical Quarterly*, vol. 31, no. 3, 1955.

Sastri, S. Anand, 'Architecture of Nalanda Remains', *Nalanda: Past and Present*, Nalanda: Nav Nalanda Mahavihara, 1977.

Saunders, Kenneth J., 'Buddhism in China: A Historical Sketch', *The Journal of Religion*, vol. 3, no. 2, 1923.

Schmithausen, Lambert, *Maitri and Magic: Aspects of the Buddhist Attitude Toward the Dangerous in Nature*, Vienna: Verlag der Österreichischen Akademie der Wissenschaften, 1997.

Schopen, Gregory, 'A Note on the "Technology of Prayer" and a Reference to a "Revolving Bookcase" in an Eleventh-Century

Indian Inscription', in *Figments and Fragments of Mahayana Buddhism in India: More Collected Papers*, ed. Gregory Schopen, Honolulu: University of Hawaii, 2005.

Schrai, Nidaullah, 'A Note on the Grey Stucco Capitals from Pataka (Swat)', *Ancient Pakistan*, vol. XXVIII, 2017.

Seherer, Bee, 'Buddhist Tantric Thealogy? The Genealogy and Soteriology of Tara', *Buddhist-Christian Studies*, vol. 38, 2018.

Sengupta, Gautam, 'Archaeology of Coastal Bengal', in *Tradition and Archaeology: Early Maritime Contact in Indian Ocean*, ed. H.P. Ray and J.F. Stellas, New Delhi: Manohar Publishers.

Sen, Surendra Nath, *Early Career of Kanhoji Angria & Other Papers*, Calcutta: University of Calcutta, 1941.

Sengupta, R., 'Stuccos in Central Asia and India: A Reappraisal', *Puratattva*, vol. 12, 1981.

Shanmugam, P., *India and Southeast Asia: South Indian Cultural Links with Indonesia*, in *Nagapattinam to Suvarnadvipa: Reflections on the Chola Naval Expeditions to Southeast Asia*, ed. Hermann Kulke, K. Kesavapany, and Vijay Sakhuja, New Delhi: ISEAS and Manohar, 2009.

Sharma, Bajnath, *Harsha and His Times*, Varanasi: Sushma Prakashan, 1970.

Sharma, C.D., *A Critical History of Indian Philosophy*, Delhi: Motilal Banarsidass, 1997.

Sharma, R.S., 'Notes on Icons and Religious Movements in Early Medieval India', *Proceedings of the Indian History Congress*, 1998.

Shastri D.N.: The Philosophy of Nyaya Vaisesika and its Conflict with the Buddhist Dinnaga School (Critique of Indian Realism) Bhartiya Vidya Prakashan, New Delhi, (2n ed.), 1976.

Shastri, M.V., *Vaidya Yoga Ratnavali*, Madras: IMPCOPS, 1968.

Shaw, Julia, *Buddhist Landscape in Central India: Sanchi Hill and Archaeology of Religion and Social Changes, Third Century BC to Fifth Century AD*, London: The British Academy, 2007.

Shaw, Sarah, 'Yasodhara in Jataka', *Buddhist Studies Review*, 35.1-2, 2018.

Schopen, G., Bones, Stones and Buddhist Monks, Honolulu, 1997.

Schopenhauer, Arthur The World as Will and Representation(vol.1) United States, Echo Point Books & Media, 2021.

Sen, A.C., Rajagriha and Nalanda (2nd edn.), Calcutta: Indian Publicity Society, 1964.

Shastri, D.N., The Philosophy of Nyaya-Vaiṣeṣika and its Conflict with Buddhist Dignaga School, BharatiyaVidyaBhavan, 1976.

Singh, Anand, *Nalanda: A Glorious Past*, Primus Books, 2024.

Singh, Anand, *Destruction and Decline of Nālandā Mahāvihāra: Prejudices and Praxis*, Sri Lanka: Royal Asiatic Society, 2023.

Singh, Jaideva (ed.), Conception of Buddhist Nirvana of Stcherbatsky, Delhi: Motilal Banarsidass, 1977.

Singh, Jaideva, *Introduction to Madhyamaka Philosophy*, Varanasi, India: Bharatiya Vidya Prakashan, 1968.

Singh, Purushottam, 'The Neolithic Culture of Northern and Eastern India', *Prehistory: Archaeology of South Asia*, Delhi: Manohar, 2002.

Singh, R.L., *India, A Regional Geography*, Varanasi: National Geographic Society of India, 2015.

Skilton, Andrew, *"How the Nagas Were Pleased" by Harsa and "The Shattered Thighs" by Bhasa*, New York: New York University Press, 2009.

Smith, Monica L., 'Indianization from Indian Point of View: Trade and Cultural Contacts with Southeast Asia in Early First Millennium CE', *Journal of the Economic and Social History of the Orient*, 1999.

Smith, Vincent A., Early History of India: from 600 B.C. to the Mohammadan Conquest, Oxford: 1906, ASIAR,1924-25.

Snellgrove, David L., *The Hevajra Tantra: A Critical Study*, Oxford: Oxford University Press, 1980.

Snodgrass, Adrian, *The Symbolism of the Stupa*, Delhi: Motilal Banarsidass, 2007.

Srivastava, K.M., *Excavation at Piprahwa and Ganwaria*, New Delhi: ASI, 1996.

Staszczyk, Agnieszka, 'Goat-Headed Deities in Ancient Indian Sculpture', *Art of the Orient*, vol. 9, 2020.

Stchebatsky T.: Buddhist Logic, vol.I and 2, Dover Publications Inc, New York, 1962.

Steavu, Dominic, 'Apotropaic Substances as Medicine in Buddhist Healing Methods, Nagarjuna's Treatise on the Five Sciences', in *Buddhism and Medicine: An Anthology of Pre-Modern Sources*, New York: Columbia University Press, 2017.

Steinkellner, E., 'Methodological Remarks on the Constitution of Sanskrit Texts from the Buddhist Pramana-Tradition', *Wiener Zeitschrift für die Kunde Südasiens und Archiv für indische Philosophie*, vol. 32, 1988.

Stewart, Mary L., *Nalanda Mahavihara: A Critical Analysis of the Archaeology of an Indian Buddhist Site*, Delhi: 2018.

Stcherbatsky, Theodore, *Buddhist Logic*, Delhi: Munshiram Manoharlal, 2 vols., 1996.

Strauch, Ingo, 'The Evolution of the Buddhist Raksa Genre in the Light of New Evidence from Gandhara: The Manasvi-Nagaraja-Sutra from the Bajaur Collection of Kharosthi Manuscripts', *Bulletin of SOAS*, 2014.

Suzuki, Takayasa, 'Rites and Buddhism: A Perspective from the Sarasvatiparivarta in the Surana Prabhasa', *Journal of Indian and Buddhist Studies*, vol. 52, no. 2, 2004.

Takakusu, Juajiro, *I-Isingh: A Record of the Buddhist Religion as Practiced in India and the Malay Archipelago, AD 671-695*, Delhi: Munshiram Manoharlal, 1998, reprint.

Tatelman, Joel, *The Trails of Yasodhara and the Birth of Rahula: A Synopsis of Bhadrakalapavadān II-IX*, Buddhist Studies Review, vol. 15, no. 1, 1998.

Tatz, Mark, *Buddhism and Healing*: Demieville's article *'Byo'* from *Hobogirin*, New York: University Press of America, 1985.

Latz, Mark, *The Life of Candragomin in Tibetan Historical Tradition*, The Tibetan Journal, vol. 7, no. 3, 1982.

Thapa, S., "Transmission of Indian Buddhist Thought in East Asian Historiography: Dhyānabhadra (Chi-Gong) and Buddhism in 14th Century Korea", Sixth World Korean Studies Congress, 2006.

Thapar, Romila, *From Lineage to State: The Evolution of State in the Ganga Valley in the Mid First Millennium BCE*, Cultural Past, ed. Romila Thapar, Delhi: Oxford University Press, 2000.

Thaplyal, K.K., *Studies in Ancient Indian Seals*, Lucknow: Akhila Bharatiya Sanskrit Parishad, 1972.

Thera, Nyanaponika, *The Life of Shariputra*, Kandy: Buddhist Publication Society, 2008.

Thomas, Henry Harrington, *The Late Rebellion in India and Our Future Policy*, London: W Kind, 1908.

Thomas, E.J., *History of Buddhist Thought*, Routledge and Kegan Paul, London, (2nd ed.), 1951.

Tiwary, Sachin Kumar, and Shubham Saurabh, "Archaeological Evidences of Toilet System in Ancient India", *Heritage: Journal of Multidisciplinary Studies in Archaeology*, vol. 6, 2018.

Tom J.F. Tillemans, *Scripture, Logic, Language: Essays on Dharmakirti and His Tibetan Successors*, Wisdom Publications, 1999.

Trainer, Kevin, *Relics, Ritual and Representation in Buddhism*, Cambridge, 1997.

Tripathi, Radhavallabh, *Vada in Theory and Practice: Studies in Debate, Dialogues and Discussions in Indian Intellectual Discourses*, Delhi: D.K. Printworld, 2016.

Tripathi, Sila, "Seafaring Archaeology of the East Coast of India and Southeast Asia during the Early Historical Period", *Ancient Asia*, vol. 8, no. 7, 2017.

Tripathi, Radhavallabh, *Makers of Indian Literature: Dharmakirti*, New Delhi: Sahitya Akademi, 2014.

Tucci, Giuseppe, "A Fragment from the *Pratitya-samutpada-vyakhya* of Vasubandhu", *The Journal of the Royal Asiatic Society of Great Britain and Ireland*, 1930.

Upasak, C.S. (ed.), *Nalanda: Past and Present*, Nalanda: Nava Nalanda Mahavihara, 1977.

Vaidya, P.L. (ed.), *Karandavyuha Sutra*, in *Mahayana-sutra-samgraha*, Part 1: Buddhist Sanskrit Texts No. 17, Darbhanga: The Mithila Institute of Post-Graduate Studies and Research, 1961.

Van Leur, I.C., *Indonesian Trade and Society: Essays in Asian Social and Economic History*, Selected Studies on Indonesia by Dutch Scholars, vol. I, Amsterdam: W. Van Hoeve Ltd., The Hague, Bandung, published for the Royal Tropical Institute, vol. 1, 1955.

Vajirā, Sister & Story, Francis, Last Days of the Buddha: Maha-parinibbana Sutta, Sri Lanka, Buddhist Publication Society, 2007.

Varma, K.M., Stucco in India, Santiniketan: Nabajiban Press, 1983.

Venkata Ramanan, K., Nagarjuna's Philosophy, Delhi: Motilal Banarsidass, 1978.

Vidyabhusana, Satis Chandra, 'Dignaga and His Pramana-samuccaya', Journal of Asiatic Society of Bengal, vol. 1, no. 9, 1905.

Vidyabhushan, S.C., History of Indian Logic, New Delhi: Motilal Banarsidass, 1978

Vogel. J.Ph., Indian Serpent Lore or the Nagas in Hindu Legend and Art, New Delhi: Gyan Publishing House, 2021, reprint.

Waddell, L.A., The Buddhism of Tibet or Lamaism, London, Gaurav Publishing House,1985.

Walser, Joseph, *Nagarjuna in Context: Mahayana Buddhism and Early Indian Culture*, Delhi: Motilal Banarsidass.

Walker, Benjamin, *Hindu World: An Encyclopedic Survey of Hinduism*, London: Allen and Unwin, 1968.

Wallace, Vesna, *A Diverse Aspects of Its Mongolian Buddhist Manuscript Culture and Realms of Its Influence*, in *Buddhist London*, New York, 2009.

Waley, Arthur, *New Light on Buddhism in Medieval India*, 1931-1932.

Walters, Thomas, On Yuan Chwang's Travel in India (629–645 CE), Vol. II, New Delhi, 2004.

Walleser, Max, *The Life of Nagarjuna from Tibetan and Chinese Sources*, New Delhi: Asian Educational Services, 1990.

Warmington, E.H., *The Commerce Between Roman Empire and India*, Delhi: Vikas Publishing House, 1974.

Waymann, A.: The rules of Debate According to Asanga, Journal of American Oriental Society, Vol. 78 (1958), pp. 29–40

Warren, Henry Clarke, Buddhism in Translations, Harvard University Press, 1896.

Wedemeyer, Christian, Vajrayana and its Doubles: The Tantric Works of Aryadeva, University of Michigan: Microfilm Services, 2000.

Westerhoff, Jan, *The Golden Age of Indian Buddhist Philosophy*, Oxford: Oxford University Press, 2018.

Williams, Joanna, G. (ed.), The Art of Gupta India Empire and Province, New Delhi: Heritage Publications, 1983.

Williams, Paul, *Mahayana Buddhism: The Doctrinal Foundations*, London: Routledge, 1989.

Winternitz, Maurice, *A History of Indian Literature*, New Delhi: Oriental Books Reprint Corporation, 1977.

Xiang, Wang, 'From Nalanda to Chang'an: A Survey of Buddhist Libraries in Medieval China (618-907)', in Tansen Sen (ed.), *Buddhism across Asia: Networks of Material, Intellectual and Cultural Exchange*, Singapore, 2014.

Xuanzang, *The Great Tang Dynasty Record of the Western Regions*, trans. Li Rongxi, Berkeley, 1996.

Yun-hua, Jon, 'Nagarjuna One or More? A New Interpretation of Buddhist Hagiography', *History of Religions*, vol. 10, no. 2, 1970.

Zurcher, Erik, *The Buddhist Conquest of China*, Leiden: Brill, 1972.

Zysk, Kenneth G., *Asceticism and Healing in Ancient India, Medicine in the Buddhist Monastery*, New Delhi: Motilal Banarsidass, 2000.

Endnotes

Introduction

1   Frederick M. Asher, *Nalanda: Situating the Great Monastery*, Marg Publication, Delhi, 2008, pg.8
2   'Excavated Remains of Nalanda Mahavihara', ASI, Ministry of Culture, GOI Nomination Dossier for UNESCO WHS pg.16 https://whc.unesco.org/uploads/nominations/1502.pdf
3   Shaman Hwui Li, *The Life of Hiuen-Tsiang*, trans. Beal Samuel 1911 pg.159
4   Rene Grousset, *In the Footsteps of the Buddha*, Routledge and K. Paul, 1971 translated by Mariette Leon
5   William Dalrymple, *The Golden Road*, Bloomsbury, 2024 Pg.131
6   'Excavated Remains of Nalanda Mahavihara', ASI, Ministry of Culture, GOI Nomination Dossier for UNESCO WHS pg.16 https://whc.unesco.org/uploads/nominations/1502.pdf
7   'Excavated Remains of Nalanda Mahavihara', ASI, Ministry of Culture, GOI Nomination Dossier for UNESCO WHS pg.40 https://whc.unesco.org/uploads/nominations/1502.pdf

1. Nalanda: A Suburb of Rajagriha, the First Capital of Magadha

1 *Last Days of the Buddha: Maha-parinibbana Sutta*, Translated from the Pali by Sister Vajira and Francis Story, Buddhist Publication Society, 2007, pg.6

2 Excerpt from SN 8.6 *Sariputtasutta*

3 'Rajgir', Nekhor, 13 November 2024, https://www.nekhor. org/buddha/rajgir

4 ibid

5 Arthur Schopenhauer, *The World as Will and Representation*, 1819, Volume 1, § 71

6 Isaak Jacob Schmidt, 'On the Mahâjâna and Prajnâ-Pâramita of the Buddha'. In: *Mémoires de l'Académie imperiale des sciences de St. Pétersbourg*, VI, 4, 1836, 145-149

7 Hwui Li, *The life of Hiuen Tsang*, Translated by Samuel Beal, 1914, London. Kegan Paul, Trench, Trubner & Co. Ltd.

8 A philosophical system of Indian materialism which believes in maximization of one's own pleasure and rejects supernaturalism including soul or God

9 The book title means a hundred deeds, is a collection of 120 Avadanas. Each Avadana tells a story that ends with the Buddha explaining what happened in terms of Karma

2. Nalanda's Legendary Sons: Shariputra and Maudgalyayana

1 N. Thera and H. Hecker, *Great Disciples of the Buddha*, ed. By Bikkhu Bodhi, Wisdom Publication, 2003

2 The fourth book of *Vinaya Pitaka* (the first of three *Pitakas*), the definitive canonical collection of scriptures of Theravada Buddhism

3 A. Bareau, *Devadatta and the First Buddhism Schism*. Buddhist Studies Review, 14 (1), 19-37, 1997

3. The Rise of Nalanda Mahavihara

1 'Excavated Remains of Nalanda Mahavihara', ASI, Ministry of Culture, GOI Nomination Dossier for UNESCO WHS pg.16 https://whc.unesco.org/uploads/nominations/1502.pdf

2 Hwui Li, *The life of Hiuen Tsang*, Translated by Samuel Beal, 1914, London. Kegan Paul, Trench, Trubner & Co. Ltd.

3 Butea Frondosa

4 Sourced from an epigraph dating from the mid-eighth century, recording a donation made by Mālāda, son of Tikina, minister of Yaśovarman of Kanauj, found at the Barāgon site. 'Excavated Remains of Nalanda Mahavihara', ASI, Ministry of Culture, GOI Nomination Dossier for UNESCO WHS pg.17-18 https://whc.unesco.org/uploads/nominations/1502.pdf

5 Hwui Li, *The life of Hiuen Tsang*, Translated by Samuel Beal, 1914, London. Kegan Paul, Trench, Trubner & Co. Ltd. pg. 112

6 Frederick Asher, *Situating the Great Monastery*, Marg Publication, Delhi, 2008

7 'Property: Excavated Remains of Nalanda Mahavihara', ASI, Ministry of Culture, GOI Nomination Dossier for UNESCO WHS pg. 27 https://whc.unesco.org/uploads/nominations/1502.pdf

8 Ibid pg. 27

9 Ibid.

10 Ibid pg.26

11 Ibid pg. 26

12 Ibid pg. 27

13 Ibid pg 27 based on studies of (Cunningham, 2000) (Ghosh, 2006) (Phuoc, 2010)(Kamini, Kulkarni, Raghavaswamy, & Roy, 2007)(Misra, 2008).

14 Ibid pg.30

15 Ibid pg.29

16 Hwui Li, *The Life of Xuanzang*, Translated by Samuel Beal, 1914, London. Kegan Paul, Trench, Trubner & Co. Ltd. pg. 112

17 Frederick M. Asher, *Nalanda: Situating the Great Monastery*, Marg Foundation, 2015, pg.

18 Xuanzang, *Buddhist Records of the Western Countries*, translated by S. Beal book IX, P-171

19 Thomas Watters (1904). 'On Yuan Chwang's Travels in India 629-645 AD', *Royal Asiatic Society*, London, Vol II- P-168

20 *Early Aryans to Swaraj, Indian Education and Rajputs*, Ed. by Dr. S.R. Bakshi, Dr. S. Gajrani, Dr. Hari Singh, Sarup & Sons, New Delhi, 2005, Volume -3 pg. 221

21 Xuanzang, *Buddhist Records of the Western Countries*, translated by Samuel Beal, Book IX, pg. 170

22 Hwui Li, *The Life of Hiuen-Tsiang*, Translated by Samuel Beal, 1914, London. Kegan Paul, Trench, Trubner & Co. Ltd. pg. 112

23 Hwui Li, *The Life of Hiuen-Tsiang*, Translated by Samuel Beal, 1914, London. Kegan Paul, Trench, Trubner & Co. Ltd. pg. 112

24 I-tsing, *A Record of the Buddhist Religion*, trans.J.Takakusu, p.86.

25 ibid

26 I-tsing, *A Record of Buddhist Practices*, trans.J.Takakusu, Ch. XX, pg. 108

27 Takakusu's A Record of Buddhist Religion, Pg.84

28 I-tsing, *A Record of Buddhist Practices*, trans.J.Takakusu, Ch. XX, pg. 108

29 Dutt, Sukumukar, The University of Nalanda, Nalanda: Giver of Wisdom and Bridge of Friendship, Embassy of India, Beijing, 2009, pg. 124

4. The Luminaries of Nalanda

1   I-Tsing, *Nan-hae-k' i-kwei-nin-f d-ch'uen*, referred to by Samuel Beal, /. R, A. 5., XIII (N. S.), p. 571.

2   Taranath, *History of Buddhism in India*, trans. Lama Chimpa and Alaka Chattopadhyay, Motilal Banarsidass Publishers, New Delhi 1970 p. 167

3   Taranath, *History of Buddhism in India*, trans. Lama Chimpa and Alaka Chattopadhyay, Motilal Banarsidass Publishers, New Delhi 1970 p. 167-168

4   Ibid pg. 171

5   Ibid pg. 167

6   'Nalanda: The university that changed the world' by Sugato Mukherjee 2023 https://www.bbc.com/travel/article/20230222-nalanda-the-university-that-changed-the-world

7   Ibid pg.51

8   H.D. Sankalia, *Pandits of Nalanda*, University of Nalanda 1934 ed. P. 105

9   A Hindu linguist philosopher of sixth century CE and the writer of influential work of Sanskrit poetry *Satakatrayam*

10 I Tsing, *A Record of Buddhist Practices*, trans. By J. Takasuku, Cosmo Pub, New Delhi 2006, pg. 180

11 Hwui Li, *Life of Hiuen-Tsiang*, trans. By Samuel Beal, London, p. 160

12 H.D. Sankalia, *Pandits of Nalanda*, University of Nalanda 1934 ed. Pg. 110

13 Octavio Paz, *In Light of India*, trans by Eliot Weinberger, Harcourt Brace and Company, New York, 1997 pg. 142

14 William Dalrymple, *The Golden Road*, Bloomsbury, 2024 p. 192

15 L. A. Waddell, *Buddhism of Tibet or Lamaism*, W.H. Allen &Co. London, 1895, pg 24-28.

16 Dziwenka, Ronald James (2010). "'The last light of Indian Buddhism'—The monk Zhikong in 14th century China and Korea (PhD dissertation)". The University of Arizona.

17 Thapa, S (2006). "Transmission of Indian Buddhist Thought in East Asian Historiography: Dhyānabhadra (Chi-Gong) and Buddhism in 14th Century Korea". Sixth World Korean Studies Congress.

18 Waley, Arthur, New Light on Buddhism in Medieval India, Melanges chinois et bouddhiques Vol. 1931-1932, Juillet 1932, P.355-376

5. Foreign Scholars at Nalanda

1 Fahien, *A Record of the Buddhist Kingdoms*, trans by James Legge, Clarendon Press, Oxford, 1886, Ch.III, pg. 16-17

2 ibid pg.99-100

3 ibid pg. 81

4 H.D. Sankalia, *The Rise of the University, University of Nalanda* 1934, Ch-III, pg. 38–40

5 Hwui Li, *The Life of Hiuen-Tsiang*, Translated by Samuel Beal, 1914, London. Kegan Paul, Trench, Trubner & Co. Ltd. pg.105-106

6 Ibid pg.106-107

7 During Tang Dynasty one Sheng was equivalent to 594 milliliters

8 S-C Shiu and H-O Chien, 'The Educational System of Nalanda from Chinese Records,' in *The Heritage of Nalanda* ed. By C. Mani, Pg 193.

9 Hwui Li, *The Life of Hiuen-Tsiang*, Translated by Samuel Beal, 1914, London. Kegan Paul, Trench, Trubner & Co. Ltd. pg.121

10 V.V.S. Saibaba, 'Nalanda's contribution to the Chinese Buddhist Philosophical Literature,' in *Contribution of Nalanda to World Culture* ed. b y Ravindra Panth, 2009, pg 10.

11 I Tsing, *A Record of Buddhist Practices*, trans. By J. Takasuku, Cosmo Pub, New Delhi 2006, Introduction pg. 19

12 Name of a peak in Mountain Sung in Honan where many of I Tsing's friends lived

13 I Tsing, *A Record of Buddhist Practices*, trans. By J. Takasuku, Cosmo Pub, New Delhi 2006, pg. 215

14 Yijing, *Memoirs of Eminent Monks who Visited India and Neighboring Regions in Search on the Law during the Great Tang Dynasty*, translated by Lahiri, Latika, Motilal Banarasidas, New Delhi, 1986

15 ibid

6. The Decline of Nalanda

1   Dr. Babashaeb Ambedkar: *The Decline and Fall of Buddhism, Writings and Speeches* Volume III, ed by Vasant Moon, Dr. Ambedkar Foundation, New Delhi, 2014 pg. 230

2   Ibid pg 229-230

3   As per Dutt, *Buddhist Monks and Monasteries of India*, 1962, Prof. P.V. Bapat, 1956, Phuoc, Buddhist Architecture, 2010.

4   William Dalrymple, *The Golden Road*, Bloomsbury, 2024 pg. 279

5   Singh Anand, Nalanda: A Glorious Past, Decline and Destruction, Primus Books, 2024, Pg. 505-506

6   ibid pg. 507

7   ibid pg. 508

8   H. M. Elliot and John Dowson, *The History of India As Told by Its Own Historians*, London:Trubner, vol.II:306 (Bakhtiyar's capture of Odantapur (Uddandapur) vihār has

been synchronized with that of Kalinjar of Aibak which is dated 1203 CE by Hasan Nizami in his *Tajul Maasir*).

9   Jamphel Shonu, 'Situating the Great Monastery of Nalanda through the Asher Archive,' https://aims.vmis.in/caa-exhibitions/exhibition/situating-the-great-monastery-of-nalanda-through-the-asher-archive/ accessed on 2 June 2024

10   Anand Singh, '"Destruction" and "Decline" of Nalanda Mahavihara: Prejudices and Praxis', *Journal of Royal Asiatic Society*, Sri Lanka branch, 2023, pg. 23

11   ibid pg.27-28

12   Ibid pg. 28 and H.M. Elliot and John Dowson, *The History of India as Told by Its Own Historians*, London: Trubner Vol. Ill, 1867–1877 (reprint 1996)

13   Taranatha, *History of Buddhism in India*, translated by Lama, Chimpa and Chattopadhyaya, A., Shimla: Indian Institute of Advanced Studies, 1970:319-320

14   George Roerich, *Biography of Dhammasvāmī (Chag Lo tsa-baChos- rje-dpal)*, Patna, K.P. Jaiswal Research Institute, 1959:62-63

15   Arthur Waley, *New Light on Buddhism in Medieval India, Mélanges Chinois et bouddhique*, 1932:355-376

16   William Dalrymple, *The Golden Road*, Bloomsbury, 2024 pg. 279

17   Hemachandra Raychaudhury, *Political History of Ancient India, University of Calcutta*, 1972:235-236

18   Anand Singh, '"Destruction" and "Decline" of Nalanda Mahavihara: Prejudices and Praxis', *Journal of the Royal Asiatic Society of Sri Lanka*, New Series, Vol. 58, No. 1 (2013), pg.35

19   Dr S. Radhakrishnan, *Indian Philosophy*, George Allen & Unwin Ltd. London, 1923

20   Daya Krishna, *Was Acārya Śaṅkara Responsible For the Disappearance of Buddhist Philosophy in India*, New Delhi,2001: pg.166-167

21 R. K. Dasgupta, *Vedanta in Bengal,* Calcutta, Ramakrishna Mission, 2003: pg. 3-5

22 K. T. S Sarao, *The Decline of Buddhism in India: A Fresh Perspective,* New Delhi, Munishram Manoharlal Publishers, 2012: pg.89

23 Anand Singh, '"Destruction" and "Decline" of Nalanda Mahavihara: Prejudices and Praxis,'

24 M. Monier-Williams, *Buddhism,* 1995, pg.165-166

25 Anand Singh, '"Destruction" and "Decline" of Nalanda Mahavihara: Prejudices and Praxis,' pg.40 and Bimlendru Mohanty, *Buddhist Heritage of Orissa (From Kalinga to Sri Lanka),* New Delhi, Vohra Publications, 2009: pg. 63-65

26 Pag Sam Jon Zang, 122, R. C. Majumdar, *History of Bengal,* 1943:344

27 Thomas Walters, *On Yuan Chwang's Travel in India (629–645 CE), Vol. II,* New Delhi, 2004pg. 164

28 Shaman Hwui Li, *The Life of Hiuen-Tsiang,* trans. Beal Samuel 1911pg. 159

29 *Epigraphia Indica,* Vol. IX (1907-1908):320-321

7. Nalanda's Contributions: How It Changed the World

1 *Nomination Dossier: Property: Excavated Remains of Nalanda Mahavihara,* UNESCO World Heritage Centre, pg. 128 https://whc.unesco.org/uploads/nominations/1502.pdf

2 *Nomination Dossier: Property: Excavated Remains of Nalanda Mahavihara,* UNESCO World Heritage Centre, pg. 22 pg.

3 Bapat, Prof. P.V., Dutt, 1962, Mookerji, 1974

4 F. R. Allchin and George Erdosy (1995). *The Archaeology of Early Historic South Asia: The Emergence of Cities and States.* Cambridge University Press. pp. 247–249. ISBN 978-0-521-37695-2.

5   Johannes Bronkhorst (2011). *Buddhism in the Shadow of Brahmanism*. Brill Academic. pp. 96–97 with footnotes.

6   Harle, 48, 54–56, 119–120; Michell, 67

7   *Britannica*, The Editors of Encyclopaedia. 'vihara'. Encyclopedia Britannica, 26 Apr. 2024, https://www.britannica.com/topic/vihara. Accessed 29 May 2024.

8   *Nomination Dossier: Property: Excavated Remains of Nalanda Mahavihara*, UNESCO World Heritage Centre, pg. 40 https://whc.unesco.org/uploads/nominations/1502.pdf

9   Christopher I. Beckwith, *Warriors of the Cloisters*, Princeton University Press, 2012, Pg.41

10 *Text, History and Philosophy, Abhidharma across Buddhist Scholastic Traditions*, ed. By Bart Dessein and Weijen Teng, Brill Academic Publications, 2016 pg. 39

11 Christopher I. Beckwith, *Warriors of the Cloisters*, Princeton University Press, 2012, Pg.41

12 William Dalrymple, *The Golden Road*, Bloomsbury, 2024, pg. 277-278

13 William Dalrymple, *The Golden Road*, Bloomsbury, 2024, pg. 277

14 Christopher I. Beckwith, *Warriors of the Cloisters*, Princeton University Press, 2012, Pg.40

15 William Dalrymple, *The Golden Road, Bloomsbury*, 2024, pg. 277

16 Christopher I. Beckwith, *Warriors of the Cloisters*, Princeton University Press, 2012, Pg.43-44

17 Ibid pg 44

18 Ibid pg.45

19 *Text, History and Philosophy, Abhidharma across Buddhist Scholastic Traditions*, ed. By Bart Dessein and Weijen Teng, Brill Academic Publications, 2016 pg. 39,

20 ibid

21 ibid

22 Sabyasachi Chatterjee, Indian Institute of Astrophysics, Hindustan Times, 20 Jan 2013

23 William Dalrymple, *The Golden Road*, Bloomsbury, 2024, p.243

24 Amartya Sen, *Nalanda: Giver of Wisdom and bridge of friendship* p.27-28

25 William Dalrymple, *The Golden Road*, Bloomsbury, 2024 p.152

26 'Nalanda and the pursuit of Science', Amartya Sen https://nextfuture.aurosociety.org/nalanda-and-the-pursuit-of-science

27 Ibid.

28 Ibid.

29 Ibid.

30 Christopher I. Beckwith, *Warriors of the Cloisters*, Princeton University Press, 2012

31 William Dalrymple, *The Golden Road*, Bloomsbury 2024, pg. 12

32 'Nomination Dossier: Property: Excavated Remains of Nalanda Mahavihara', UNESCO World Heritage Centre, pg.75 https://whc.unesco.org/uploads/nominations/1502.pdf

33 Ibid pg.75-76

34 'Nomination Dossier: Property: Excavated Remains of Nalanda Mahavihara', UNESCO World Heritage Centre, pg.110 https://whc.unesco.org/uploads/nominations/1502.pdf

35 Hwui Li, *The Life of Xuanzang*, trans. By Samuel Beal, pg.159

36 'Avinash Kumar Srivastava, 'The Contribution of the Logicians of Nalanda in the Development of Indian Logic', *Contribution of Nalanda to World Culture*, Published by Nava Nalanda Mahavihara, 2009, pg. 51

37 Ibid pg.49

38 Ibid pg.51

39 William Dalrymple, *The Golden Road*, Bloomsbury, 2024, pg.

40 'Nomination Dossier: Property: Excavated Remains of Nalanda Mahavihara', UNESCO World Heritage Centre, pg.55-56 https://whc.unesco.org/uploads/nominations/1502.pdf

41 Ibid pg.56

42 Huntington, 1984

43 Debjani Paul, *The Art of Nalanda: Development of Buddhist Sculpture A.D. 600-1200*, Munshiram Manoharlal Publishers 1995

44 'Nomination Dossier: Property: Excavated Remains of Nalanda Mahavihara', UNESCO World Heritage Centre, pg.59 https://whc.unesco.org/uploads/nominations/1502.pdf

45 Ibid pg 59

46 Ibid pg.40

47 Ibid pg. 30

48 Ibid pg. 30

49 Singh, Anand, Nalanda: A Glorious Past, 2023, pp. 455-456.

50 William Dalrymple, *The Golden Road*, Bloomsbury, 2024

51 Swati Chemburkar, (2016). Andrea Acri, (ed.). 'Borobudur's Pāla Forbear? A Field Note from Kesariya, Bihar, India'. In *Esoteric Buddhism in Mediaeval Maritime Asia; Networks of Masters, Texts, Icons*. ISEAS–Yusof Ishak Institute. pp. 191–210. ISBN 9789814695091.

52 Ibid, pg. 456-457

53 U. S. Vyas, 'Contribution of Nalanda for the Enrichment of Sanskrit Literature and National Cultures of Some of the Asian Countries', *Contributions of Nalanda to World Culture*, Nava Nalanda Mahavihara, 2009, pg. 45

54 Loizzo, *Candrakīrti and the Moonflower of Nālandā: Objectivity and Self-Correction in the Buddhist Central Philosophy of Language*, Columbia University, 2001

55 Chandra Dhar Tripathi, 'Beginnings of the Apabhramsa Poetry', *The Contribution of Nalanda, The Heritage of Nalanda*

ed. By C.S. Mani, Aryan Books International, New Delhi 2008, pg. 159

56 Chandra Dhar Tripathi, 'Beginnings of the Apabhramsa Poetry', *The Contribution of Nalanda, The Heritage of Nalanda* ed. By C.S. Mani, Aryan Books International, New Delhi 2008, pg. 158

57 Nalanda: Singh, Anand, A Glorious Past, Book Cult in Nalanda, Primus Books, 2024, Pg. 131

58 Ibid pg. 146

59 Ibid pg. 165

60 Ibid pg. 165-166

61 Ibid pg. 179

62 Ibid pg. 180-181

63 *The Golden Road* by William Dalrymple, Bloomsbury, 2024 pg.69-70

8. Many Nalandas: Nalanda's Global Footprint

1 Situating the Great Monastery of Nalanda Through the Asher Archive

2 Nava Nalanda Mahavihara website, https://www.nnm.ac.in/about-us/history/

3 Nalanda University website, Academic https://nalandauniv.edu.in/academics/

4 Sakya International Buddhist Academy, 2024, https://www.sakya.com.au/nalendra-monastery/

5 Nalanda-Sriwijaya Centre https://www.iseas.edu.sg/centres/nalanda-sriwijaya-centre/nsc-about-us/

Index

190 Index

192   Index

Scan QR code to access the
Penguin Random House India website